MURTY CLASSICAL
LIBRARY OF INDIA

Sheldon Pollock, General Editor

THERIGATHA

MCLI 3

THERIGATHA

Poems of the First Buddhist Women

Translated by
CHARLES HALLISEY

MURTY CLASSICAL LIBRARY OF INDIA
HARVARD UNIVERSITY PRESS
Cambridge, Massachusetts
London, England
2015

Printed in the United States of America

SERIES DESIGN BY M9DESIGN

Library of Congress Cataloging-in-Publication Data

Therigatha : poems of the first Buddhist women /
translated by Charles Hallisey.
p. cm. — (Murty Classical Library of India ; 3)
Includes bibliographical references and index.
ISBN 978-0-674-42773-0 (cloth : alk. paper)
1. Buddhist poetry. 2. Pali poetry—Translations into English.
I. Hallisey, Charles, 1953- translator.
BQ1452.E5H35 2015
294.3'8232—dc23 2014016313

CONTENTS

INTRODUCTION

The *Therīgāthā* is an anthology of poems by and about the first Buddhist women. These women were *therīs,* "senior ones," among ordained Buddhist women and they bore that epithet because of their religious achievements. The *therīs* in the *Therīgāthā* are enlightened women and most of the poems (*gāthā*) in the anthology are the songs of their experiences. Dhammapala, the sixth-century Buddhist commentator on the *Therīgāthā,* calls the *therīs*' poems *udāna,* "inspired utterances," and by doing so, he associated the *Therīgāthā* with a venerable Buddhist speech genre. For Dhammapala, the characteristic mark of an *udāna* was that "the utterance" would be "one or more verses consisting of knowledge about some situation accompanied by the euphoria that is felt there, for an *udāna* is proclaimed by way of a composition of verses and caused to rise up through joy and euphoria. . . ."[1]

As salt just seems to go with food, the adjective "first" and the *Therīgāthā* seem to go together. It is easy to see why. The *Therīgāthā* is an anthology of poems composed by some of the *first* Buddhists; while the poems of the *Therīgāthā* are clearly nowhere near as old as the poetry of the *Ṛg Veda,* for example, they are still some of the *first* poetry of India; the *Therīgāthā's* poems are some of the *first* poems by women in India; as a collection, the *Therīgāthā* is the *first* anthology of women's literature in the world. As such statements suggest, to use the adjective "first" is to point to something key to the value that these poems have for us. We often try to draw out that value by turning our attention to the religious, literary, and social contexts in which the poems were composed and then try to see the *Therīgāthā* as expressions of those contexts. It is important, however, to ask when we think of the poems as "first" in these different ways, whether valuing the *Therīgāthā* in such a manner may be predetermining how we approach the work. In other words, while reading and appreciating the *Therīgāthā* for being the first of so many things is no doubt appropriate, we also want to ask ourselves if seeing the *Therīgāthā* in this way also predisposes us to read the poems mainly for their historical information, and whether this might come at the expense of their expressive, imaginative, and emotional content, as well as their aesthetic achievements.

Reading the Therīgāthā as Poetry

The *Therīgāthā* is not merely a collection of historical documents to be used as evidence of the needs, aspirations, and achievements of some of the first Buddhist women. It is an anthology of *poems*. The poems vary in quality as poetry, to be sure, but some of them deserve not only the adjective "first" in a historical sense; they also deserve to be called "great" because some of them are great literature.

They are literature in the way that Ezra Pound meant when he said "Literature is news that STAYS news."[2] Some of the *Therīgāthā* do seem to be news that has stayed news, and that is part of why they are able to delight us today and why sometimes they are also able to change how we see ourselves.

The *Therīgāthā,* like literature generally, can enable us to see things that we have not seen before and to imagine things that we have not dreamed of before. When reading the poems of the *Therīgāthā,* we can experience a surprising pleasure from the clarity and truth of the epiphanies they can trigger, but perhaps more important, when we experience such epiphanies, the poems give us a chance to be free from ourselves and from our usual places in the world—at least free imaginatively—and to glimpse a different potential for ourselves in the light of that epiphany. In our day-to-day lives, we may tend to assume all too often—and dread all too often—that tomorrow will be just like today, but in the pleasures that literature affords us, we may see immediately that tomorrow does not have to be like today. Such immediacy makes free.[3] The poems in the *Therīgāthā* are about that freedom, they are *udānas,* inspired utterances about the joy of being free, but as poetry, they hold out the promise, in the pleasure that they give, of being the occasion for us making free too.

This should encourage us to try to read the poems of the *Therīgāthā* for pleasure just as much as for any sociological or historical information they may contain. How a literary text from more than two millennia ago can have the capacity to give us pleasure, to speak to us about ourselves and about our world in astonishingly fresh and insightful ways, is not easy to explain, but there is no doubt that the poems of the *Therīgāthā* have proved capable of doing so. Moreover, there is no doubt that the poems are capable of giving pleasure in translation.

This was probably the case throughout the long reception

history of the *Therīgāthā*. The imprint of linguistic difference and translation seems intrinsic to the poems as we receive them, especially in the textual difficulties and linguistic peculiarities that many of the verses present. Individual poems were composed over the course of a considerable period of time, perhaps centuries; according to Buddhist tradition, they date from the time of the Buddha himself, while according to modern historical methods, some date as late as the end of the third century B.C.E.[4]

The poems as we receive them are in the Pali language, the scholarly and religious language distinctive to the Theravadin Buddhist traditions that are now found in Sri Lanka and Southeast Asia; in the first millennium, however, Theravada Buddhism was quite prominent in south India as well. It is sometimes said that originally Pali was the vernacular of a particular region of ancient India, but this seems unlikely in any simple way. Rather the Pali language was something of a "perfected language," changed in ways analogous to how Sanskrit was refined as a language. Although the Pali language may have been based on some vernacular, it was reworked and standardized quite significantly between the third century B.C.E. when the last of the poems in the *Therīgāthā* were composed and the sixth century C.E., when Dhammapala wrote his commentary on the *Therīgāthā* as a work in a scriptural canon. It seems very likely that these poems of the first Buddhist women have been "translated" into Pali from whatever their original versions may have been in any number of ancient Indian vernaculars, and then reworked as the Pali language evolved. Pali, as the language of Theravada Buddhism, is a translocal language and the "translation" of the poems in the *Therīgāthā* into Pali was key to their wide circulation as part of the Pali canon of Theravada Buddhism.

In modern world literature, it is translation, rather than translocal languages, that is key to the circulation of literary works beyond their culture of origin, and the *Therīgāthā* has had a remarkable history of modern translations, beginning with its translation into German by Karl Eugen Neumann in 1899 and into Bangla by Bijay Chandra Majumdar in 1905.[5] The great twentieth-century Sinhala novelist Martin Wickramasinghe was quite aware of this capacity of the *Therīgāthā* to work its magic in translation. He noted in the introduction to his own Sinhala translation of some of the poems that a professor of English at Oxford had said that he was delighted as he read the *Therīgāthā* in Neumann's German translation.[6] In turn, one might assume that Wickramasinghe's own pleasure in reading the *Therīgāthā* was enriched by his reading the English translation of Caroline Rhys Davids, which he mentions in his introduction.[7] And it was this that inspired him in turn to translate some of them into Sinhala, as he spoke about in the first paragraphs of his book, *Tēri gī:*

> I used to get great pleasure from the poetry in *Guttila,*[8] but now I get the same pleasure from the *Therīgāthā*. Whenever I was troubled or distressed, the poetry in *Guttila* eased my mind; whenever my mind shined with happiness, *Guttila* increased the happiness. On the many occasions that I was happy just being lazy, it was usually to *Guttila* that my hand reached out and I would

> read whatever caught my eye wherever I happened to open the book.
>
> That satisfaction and comfort that I used to get from *Guttila,* I now get from some of the verses of the Buddhist nuns. The songs, which have a deep meaning, were first played on the *vīṇās* that were the hearts of the *therīs*. They had been disappointed in life, whether after enduring suffering or enjoying pleasure, and they had learned how to ease their own anguish. The songs of their hearts can be heard even now by reading their poems. Because of the pleasure that my mind received from reading them, I wanted to share those songs by translating a few of them into Sinhala. There was pleasure for me even in translating these few verses into Sinhala.[9]

In the same work, Wickramasinghe gave advice to his Sinhala readers on what they should expect of themselves if they wanted to hear the songs of the *therīs*' hearts when they read the poems of the *Therīgāthā*. His advice emphasized that it is important not to hold onto one's own expectations of what religion should be or what Buddhism should teach when reading the *Therīgāthā*. Rather, he urged readers to be open to the possibility of the poems suggesting something quite different from what is conventionally expected, something that is encountered in and through the pleasure that the poems only give when they are read as poetry. For Wickramasinghe, the road to that pleasure, so basic to receiving the deep meaning of the *Therīgāthā,* would open up for a reader if she took the time "to remember that these verses must be read with a sensibility that is guided by the poetry itself."[10]

What does a "sensibility guided by poetry itself" look like, and how might it be brought to bear when reading the *Therīgāthā*? Taking the first verse from the poem of Ambapali as a case study can help us see how to read the poems of the *Therīgāthā* in the way Wickramasinghe commends to us, can help us anticipate the kind of richness and pleasure that comes when we take the *Therīgāthā* seriously as poetry:

kāḷakā bhamaravaṇṇasādisā vellitaggā mama
muddhajā ahuṃ
te jarāya sāṇavākasādisā saccavādivacanaṃ
anaññathā.

The hairs on my head were once curly,
black, like the color of bees,
now because of old age
they are like jute.

It's just as the Buddha, speaker of truth, said,
nothing different than that.

If we read this verse with an eye primarily for the information that it conveys, we could justifiably say that this poem is about the central Buddhist teaching on impermanence. In Buddhist thought, impermanence is one of the three marks (*tilakkhaṇa*) of the world, along with suffering (*dukkha*) and the lack of an enduring essence (*anattā*): everything in this world, including our bodies, disappoints us and causes us to suffer because everything changes in ways we do not want; everything changes because everything in the world is impermanent (*anicca*); and everything is impermanent because everything in the world lacks an enduring essence that would allow it to persist without changing. The lack of an enduring essence is particularly important to note with respect to persons, since humans are commonly prone to think otherwise, even going so far to think that we are defined by our souls (or to put it in Sanskrit, we are defined by an *ātman,* which is exactly what the Buddhist category of *anātman* [Sanskrit; in Pali, *anattā*] denies). As Susan Murcott puts it, "Ambapali's poem, while not a formal meditation—as for instance the meditation on the thirty-two parts of the body—similarly seeks to bring the image of impermanence into focus."[11] All of this is important to know about the verse, but to leave it at that is to reduce the poem to ideas that we expect a piece of Buddhist writing to teach.

Reading the verse with a sensibility guided by poetry itself encourages us to explore how the verse also brings a quite different image into view. To prepare ourselves to be able to see that image, we should first remind ourselves that poetry thrives, as T. S. Eliot said, on the "contrast between fixity and flux, this unperceived evasion of monotony, which is the very life of verse."[12]

This contrast "which is the very life of verse," the tension between expected pattern and delightful surprise in actual instance, is encountered at different levels of significance in Ambapali's poem. It is encountered quite concretely in the use of the same meter throughout the poem. The prominence of meter in classical Indian poetry meant that there was always a tension over how to use language set in predictable patterns of meter in ways that it can evade monotony in individual poems. Only when there was "this unperceived evasion of monotony" could a poem be a source of surprise and pleasure for a reader, rather than a mere occasion to admire the sterile cleverness of a poet.[13]

Ambapali's poem is in a meter that would later come to be called *rathoddhatā* in classical Sanskrit metrics, although at the time it was used in Ambapali's poem, the large schema of meters had not yet been formalized in Indian literary cultures. With poetry in the Pali language from the period in which the poems of the *Therīgāthā* were composed, we sometimes have the feeling that the literary features of what we are reading are still close to the time of their invention; as A. K. Warder said about meter in Pali poetry, "all of these Pali metres are at the very beginning of their development in the context of . . . new metrical techniques, and . . . they are the prototypes and forerunners of the magnificent repertoire of the Classical Sanskrit fixed metres."[14] Warder has also suggested that the *rathoddhatā* meter, along with some others in the *Therīgāthā,* had its origin in folk songs from that time;[15] this admittedly is speculation, but the possible musical affinities of the *rathoddhatā* meter remind us, at the very least, that poetry thrives in closeness to music.[16]

Given that we are encountering the use of this meter at an early point in the literary history of India, it is not possible to say definitively just what expectations or associations may have been set in motion for an audience when this meter was deployed in a poem. Even so, it is worth noting that in the repertoire of meters for classical Sanskrit, the *rathoddhatā* was often used for descriptions of surrounding circumstances that were thought to support and enhance the emotions of attraction and love when these were the themes of a poem. Typical surrounding circumstances for such themes were springtime and moonrise, and, with these admittedly later expectations in mind, the use of the *rathoddhatā* in Ambapali's poem appears as something of a surprise in itself. The overt theme of impermanence as seen in what aging does to a body that is central to Ambapali's poem certainly does not resonate easily with surrounding circumstances conventionally perceived as straightforwardly attractive and encouraging one to look ahead in anticipation to what is to come. That such later associations with the *rathoddhatā* meter do seem quite appropriate to bring to Ambapali's poem is reinforced by the overall structure of the poem itself, which follows a pattern also quite common in later Indian poetry in which descriptions of a woman's beauty conventionally start from the head and proceed downward in the same sequence that Ambapali uses to describe her own body.[17] The use of metaphors is, of course, one of the most visible features of poetry in India, and the first metaphor in this verse also seems suitable for a poem about attraction and love. To say that Ambapali's black hair was "the color of bees" not only describes hair color. When we take the time to see with our mind's eye what the metaphor suggests, we see not only the color of her hair, but also its texture and sheen, indeed we see the natural "movement" of her curly hair. We may feel pleasure as we imagine the beauty of the young Ambapali's hair. In meter, structure, and metaphor, Ambapali's poem thus seems to present itself within the conventions of love poetry. Naturally, we should ask to what end this would be done.

In his own discussion of this verse in *Tēri gī,* Wickramasinghe observes that there are two frameworks of perception and sentiment in Ambapali's poem, "each one trying to outdo the other." On the one hand is the framework of conventional love poetry, in which the beauties and pleasures of the body, particularly the youthful female body, are celebrated. On the other hand is the framework of conventional Buddhist descriptions of the body,[18] as noted by Murcott when describing Ambapali's poem as a meditation on the impermanence of the body. In this second framework of perception and sentiment, the body's impermanence is not to be noted in a completely affectless way. Rather, for the unenlightened, the perception of the body's impermanence generally comes with strong sentiments, sometimes of sadness, sometimes of revulsion over what happens to the body as we age, sometimes of fear from anticipating that this will inevitably happen to our own bodies.

Wickramasinghe sees the poem as putting these two contrasting frameworks of perception and sentiment into deliberate conflict with each other. He urges the readers of Ambapali's poem to try to see what she knew and felt about herself when she structured her poem around that conflict, rather than to be content to say that she was teaching a Buddhist truth about impermanence. The insight that is generated by the abiding conflict between the two frameworks of perception in the poem is not that the reality of impermanence and the fact that all of us are subject to it is sad but true. Wickramasinghe is emphatic that

> this is not the perception felt by the nun Ambapali. Rather she is saying that she once took pleasure in her hair that was black like bees but now she takes more pleasure precisely in the hair that is like jute. That nun is trying to make us savor what is real here, to see her insight and to feel her pleasure as well. That is the difference between the poetry of the *Therīgāthā* and the poetry we are used to. Other poets satisfy us with the beautiful things of this world; those poets have captured sensual things that have not been seen or perceived by us and they try to make us experience the pleasure that is to be gained through such things. What moved them then moves us.
>
> The composers of the *Therīgāthā* try to get our senses and also our hearts to grasp the things that they have seen. They do so, however, to make us experience a reality that goes beyond the reality that is known through sensory experiences of the beautiful things in this world. This is something that they do very successfully. Their vision, the vision of those who have ended their addictions to the senses, might not appeal to somebody who considers gratifying the five senses the greatest thing in the world. Someone might think that the *therīs* only detest the things of this world because they cannot have them. Even those who see things that way or think that way can receive great pleasure and insight if they read

> these *Therīgāthā* carefully, if they remain open to the *Therīgāthā* as great poetry.[19]

Wickramasinghe's attention to how the structural conflict between the two frameworks of perception helps us, as readers of the poem, to discern the delights of being free that Ambapali knew and celebrated. But it is important to emphasize that even recognizing this structural conflict depends on seeing the poem not only within the framework of Buddhist thought but also in association with nonreligious lyric poetry that focused on themes of attraction and love, without reducing the meaning of the poem to what is to be expected conventionally from either perspective. This structural conflict between the two modes of perceiving and experiencing our bodies can then generate "an unperceived evasion of monotony" in which we intuit the happiness of a freedom that is only suggested. It is a freedom from our usual ways of experiencing ourselves and it is that way of being free that Ambapali points to and celebrates in her *udāna*.

The Therīgāthā and the Pali Canon

The *Therīgāthā* is a Buddhist scripture. It is included in the Pali canon of Theravada Buddhism, in a section known as the *Khuddakanikāya* (Minor Collection), one of five parts of the *Sutta* division of the Pali canon. The Pali canon has three divisions (and thus it is called the *tipiṭaka,* "three baskets"): monastic discipline or *Vinaya,* teachings and sermons of the Buddha or *Sutta,* and abstract doctrine or *Abhidhamma*. The *Khuddakanikāya* is more heterogeneous than the other five sections of the *Suttapiṭaka,* a mix of sermons, doctrinal works, and poetry. Among the works of poetry are a separate work of *Udāna*; the *Theragāthā,* an anthology of poems by and about the first Buddhist men, which is generally paired with the *Therīgāthā*; verses about the Buddha's previous lives known as the *Jātaka;* and other important anthologies of verse like the *Dhammapada* and the *Suttanipāta*. The *Khuddakanikāya,* as a division of a Buddhist canon, seems distinctive to the Theravada and, moreover, it contains texts that are unique to that tradition. The *Therīgāthā* is one of these texts.

The broad inclusion of poetry in the *Khuddakanikāya* indicates that the poems of the *Therīgāthā* were valued as *religious* poetry by those who made the Pali canon, and this is a reminder to us that we should not overlook considering the ways in which the poems of the *Therīgāthā* could serve religious purposes. Comments made by John Ross Carter and Mahinda Palihawadana about the *Dhammapada,* an anthology of verses attributed to the Buddha, seem just as apt for the *Therīgāthā* when considering it as part of the Pali canon: "It is a religious work, meant to inculcate a certain set of religious and ethical values and a certain manner of perception of life and its problems and their solutions."[20]

Given the certain antiquity of some of the *Therīgāthā,* it is surprising that none of the individual poems has been found in what remains of the scriptural canons of the other ancient Indian Buddhist schools; nor do those canons seem to have included a textual section analogous to the *Therīgāthā*. At the same time, it is likely that some verses of the first *therīs* were not included in the *Therīgāthā* when the Theravadin canonical anthology was put together, just as some verses of the first Buddhist men were not included in the *Theragāthā*. There are a number of verses attributed to *theras,* senior male monastics, that one might have expected to be included in the *Theragāthā,* but are not found there. They are included however in two extra-canonical works, the *Milindapañha* and the *Nettipakaraṇa*—both works associated with the Gandhari Buddhist traditions of northwest India—and in Theravadin commentaries on the Pali canon. Scattered in the same works are some verses attributed to a laywoman, Chula Subhadda, parts of which bear a striking similarity to the verses attributed to Rohini in the *Therīgāthā*.[21] Referring to what she called the "unsolved puzzle of these extra-canonical verses," I. B. Horner asks whether we are "looking in the wrong place" for the sources of these verses not included in the *Theragāthā* or the *Therīgāthā*. "Perhaps, for example, we should be looking not in the Pali Canon but in the Sarvāstivāda Canon," that is, the canon of another school of early Indian Buddhism.[22]

Identifying particular *therīs* as the authors of particular poems in the *Therīgāthā* was done in the intellectual context of the still inchoate biographical traditions that were developing in various Buddhist communities in the centuries before the Common Era.[23] Just how inchoate these traditions were can be seen from the fact that some of the verses found in the *Therīgāthā* are also found in the *Saṃyuttanikāya* of the Pali canon.[24] The *Saṃyuttanikāya* is itself an anthology, and in one section it collects together verses and stories about nuns. The same verses are sometimes attributed to different *therīs* in the *Therīgāthā* than in the *Saṃyuttanikāya*.[25] It seems likely that the *Therīgāthā,* like the *Theragāthā* and the other anthologies of verses in the Pali canon, evolved over a long period of time, absorbing new poems as a collection and changing identifications of the authors of individual poems. But as the *Bhikkhunīsaṃyutta* and the verses of Chula Subhadda make clear, not all of the known poems of the first Buddhist women were included in the *Therīgāthā*.

Even though the *Therīgāthā* is part of the Pali canon, and thus scripture, the anthology and the individual poems in the anthology had a somewhat minimal reception history in the Theravada Buddhist traditions, if we take the presence of commentaries and of quotations in other works to be evidence for the later use of the *Therīgāthā's* poems; the *Therīgāthā* also seems to have had little influence on later Theravadin writing more generally. After Dhammapala's commentary on the *Therīgāthā,* no new commentaries were written on the *Therīgāthā* until perhaps the eighteenth or nineteenth centuries, when a Burmese-language gloss (*nissaya*) on the *Therīgāthā* was composed. More striking is the absence of quotations of the verses of the *Therīgāthā* in later Buddhist writing, even when the stories of *therīs* whose poems are included in the *Therīgāthā* are retold in other works, such as the *Dhammapada* commentary and its Sinhala versions.[26] On first consideration, it may look like the *Therīgāthā* as a collection of poetry by women and about women's religious experience must have been pushed to the side in the traditions of scriptural reception and interpretation in Theravada Buddhism in tandem with the decline and eventual disappearance of the order of female monastics in the Theravadin world.[27] Without discounting this possibility, however, when we keep in mind that the reception history of the comparable *Theragāthā* is not significantly different from that of the *Therīgāthā*, we might ask ourselves if we are looking in the wrong places for explanations of the relative neglect of these two collections.

With this possibility in mind, we should note that a similar fate of neglect seems to have happened to the poems of the *Therīgāthā* as literature. They do not seem to have been included in the canons of great poetry for later Buddhist literary cultures until those of the twentieth century. As poetry, the *Therīgāthā* and other Pali poetry from the same period indicate that there must have been an abrupt break between the poetic practices and values found earlier in India and evident in Vedic poetry and those of the later poetic traditions that used Middle Indic languages.[28] In this respect, what we see in the *Therīgāthā* and other early Pali poetry are best approached as precursors of what appears more fully developed in later literature in India, and especially in the Prakrit verses of Hala in his *Saṭṭasaī*, a third- or fourth-century collection of Prakrit verse. These later works show the influence of the literary forms and values that developed in the period in which the *Therīgāthā* were composed, but we do not see any evidence that the *Therīgāthā* themselves were appreciated as models of great poetry, not even in the sophisticated literary cultures of the Theravada Buddhist world. In fact, Wickramasinghe saw his own engagement with the *Therīgāthā* in the twentieth century as part of an effort to retrieve a religious and aesthetic sensibility that had been long lost to cultural and religious traditions of Sinhala Buddhism.[29]

In the materials collected in Hala's *Sattasaī,* we see a kind of poetry that is quite similar to what we find in the *Therīgāthā*. This is so with respect not only to literary forms but also to moral sensibilities. In the *Sattasaī,* we enjoy poetry in which close attention to social realities mingles with sophisticated artistic forms and with a sense of the complexities of human psychology.[30] Although we cannot say that the poetry of the *Therīgāthā* is a direct precursor to the kind of poetry we see in Hala, we do find in the *Therīgāthā* a comparable constellation of morally acute observations of social life, sophisticated artistic forms and values, and an astute awareness of human psychology.

The Therīgāthā and Early Indian Buddhism

Although the *Therīgāthā* is in Pali, a language generally restricted to Theravada Buddhist traditions, and the text is included in the Pali canon of that school of Buddhism, there is little in the *Therīgāthā's* contents, whether in doctrines or practices or institutions, that makes it distinctively Theravadin. To the contrary, the poems seem better viewed as relatively generic expressions of early Indian Buddhism. In this respect, the *Therīgāthā* is like the *Dhammapada,* although, in striking contrast to the *Therīgāthā,* other early Indian Buddhist schools seem to have their own versions of that text.

Basic Buddhist ideas common to all schools of early Buddhism are obvious in the poems of the *Therīgāthā*.

These include ideas about the nature of the world that early Buddhism shared with other Indian religions, such as the ideas of rebirth and karma (the law of moral cause and effect) that structure the conditions of experience and action for beings as they are reborn in samsara; in this general cosmology, when one does good actions then good conditions follow in this life and in future lives, including lives of pleasure in various heavens; when one does bad actions, then conditions defined by suffering and oppression inevitably follow, including lives of unspeakable misery in hells. Like other renunciant movements that were contemporary with the Buddha's, early Buddhism affirmed that a complete liberation from samsara was possible. This liberation is nirvana, and many of the *udānas* of the first Buddhist women in the *Therīgāthā* express the joy of the *therīs* at the achievement of this state of "unsurpassed safety from all that holds you back"[31] and their happiness in the knowledge that they would not be reborn again. As Isidasi says, "There is nothing better than the happiness of nibbana."[32] The poems of the *Therīgāthā* celebrate the experience of nirvana, however, rather than go into doctrinal discussions of what nirvana is.

Ideas distinctive to early Indian Buddhism are also obvious in the poems of the *Therīgāthā*. These include the Four Noble Truths that the Buddha is remembered as teaching in his first sermon, "Setting in Motion the Wheel of Truth":[33] all this is suffering; suffering has a cause; suffering can be ended; and there is a path to that end, the noble eightfold path. Also everywhere assumed in the poems of the *Therīgāthā* is the standard Buddhist redescription of a person in impersonal terms, "the dhamma about what makes a person."[34]

Instead of seeing a person in terms of a soul (*ātman*) or an enduring self or some other form of stable personal identity, early Buddhist teaching redescribed what makes a person as a concatenation of things and events: physical things, as in the body; feelings; perceptions; innate dispositions; and consciousness. These things, bundled together (*khandha*), constitute a person, each *khandha* co-dependent with the others, the parts and whole of a person constantly changing. To perceive oneself in such terms is conducive to freedom from the mental constructions that one has of oneself, and many of the meditative practices alluded to in the *Therīgāthā* are meant to cultivate such perceptions of oneself.[35] The result of learning how to see oneself in this impersonal way is expressed in Sakula's verse:

> I saw my experiences as if they were not my own,
> born from a cause, destined to disappear.
> I got rid of all that fouls the heart,
> I am cool, free.

As Sakula's reference to "all that fouls the heart" indicates, the human psychology assumed in the *Therīgāthā* is Buddhist. It is alert to how human desires, habitual mental projections, and deep unsavory dispositions are all causal factors in the ways that we construct and experience the world around us and prompts to action that bring about our own ruin and suffering. In the poetry of the *Therīgāthā,* various features of our psychology fetter us to patterns of disappointment and suffering. Most visible in the *Therīgāthā* is the awareness of features of our psychology that ooze out from within to contaminate all experiences we have of the world; these include preeminently ignorance, anger, and passion. As *udāna,* the individual verses of the *Therīgāthā* often celebrate the necessity of uprooting these dark features from human psychology, as can be seen in the following verse spoken to Tissa by the Buddha:

> Tissa, train yourself strictly, don't let
> what can hold you back overwhelm you.
> When you are free from everything that holds you back
> you can live in the world
> without the depravities that ooze out from within.

In general, the poems of the *Therīgāthā* wear their Buddhist doctrine quite lightly, and they equally avoid most specifics of Buddhist practice, whether it be the disciplinary practices of monastics or the mental training of meditators. The poems celebrate individual transformation that ends in liberation, but they give little specific instruction about how someone who wants to imitate the *therīs* might begin to undertake practices that can transform a person into what the poems celebrate. The poems obviously "inculcate a certain set of religious and ethical values and a certain manner of perception of life and its problems and their solutions," but, for the most part, they leave the specifics of doctrine and practice to other Buddhist texts.

The moral acuity of the poems of the *Therīgāthā* and their keen perception of social realities are key to appreciating the *Therīgāthā* as expressions of early Indian Buddhist life, and in this respect, the poems display religious and ethical values that are less visible in most other early Buddhist texts. While it is often the case that Buddhist sources give more information about a generic "folk religion" of early India than do Vedic and Brahmanical texts, an indication that Buddhists may have been more closely in touch with popular strata of Indian society than other religious movements, this is not especially visible in the *Therīgāthā*. We discern the distinctive moral acuity of the *Therīgāthā* and its sense of social realities elsewhere.

A good place to start, albeit a surprising one, is with the anthology's arrangement itself. The surface arrangement of poems in the *Therīgāthā* looks arbitrary, with poems grouped together into sections (*nipāta*) according to the number of verses in each poem. Other rationales for the placing of poems in the anthology seem to be at work, however, including themes based on commonality of experience and actual personal relationships between *therīs*. One of the most poignant examples of thematic links between poems that suggest a moral perception of social realities in the *Therīgāthā* are the poems of mothers who have had their own children die.[36] We also see poems grouped together that suggest the moral importance of social relationships between women, such as friendships that endure the transition between lay life and ordained life and the enduring relationships between female teachers and their female students.[37]

The community of women depicted in the *Therīgāthā* is less a single monastic order governed by a single rule (*vinaya*), than a collocation of smaller groups of women bound together by shared experiences and relationships of care and intimacy with each other, as is expressed in a verse of Rohini's poem:

> Those who have gone forth
> are from various families and from various regions
> and still they are friendly with each other—
> that is the reason why
> ascetics are so dear to me.

This valuing of relationships may explain the placement of Therika's verse as the first poem insofar as Therika's name itself suggests the significance of women living together in mutual care and intimacy. The importance of female charismatic teachers is also obvious throughout the *Therīgāthā,* while the monastic codes found in the canonical *Vinaya* are not highlighted at all. This is clearly an idealized perception of social realities, but it is no less keen. The world of the ordained women in the *Therīgāthā* is one of sexual equality, in stark contrast to the social inequalities between men and woman in lay life. It is a keen insistence on the possibility of freedom for women as well as for men.

This is especially obvious in the celebration of attainment with the declaration of "knowing the three things that most don't know." This is *tevijjā* in Pali, the ability to know one's past lives, the ability to know where and why other beings are reborn, and the ability to know that one's own moral corruptions—"all that holds one back"—have been eliminated. To know the three things that most do not know is to know that one is enlightened and that one will not be reborn. The notion of *tevijjā* in early Buddhism explicitly triggers association with ideas in Brahmanical Hinduism about *trayī vidyā,* knowledge of the three Vedas. When the *therīs* declare that they know the three things that most do not know, they are not only making a joyful affirmation of the attainment, they are rejecting Brahmanical assumptions that no woman of any caste was capable of attaining "the three knowledges."[38]

The moral acuity of the poems of the *Therīgāthā* and their keen perception of social realities may be one factor for the wide appeal that the *Therīgāthā* has had for modern readers around the world. As noted earlier, the *Therīgāthā* is one of only a few Pali works that have entered the canons of modern world literature in numerous translations. The attention given to social realities in the *Therīgāthā* always includes the endless varieties of social suffering endured by women, of course, but also those endured by the poor, as in the following poem by Chanda in which it is clear that she decides to ordain as a Buddhist nun not out of any spiritual aspiration but as a way of getting food:

> In the past, I was poor, a widow, without children,
> without friends or relatives, I did not get food or
>   clothing.
>
> Taking a bowl and stick, I went begging from family
>   to family,
> I wandered for seven years, tormented by cold and
>   heat.

> Then I saw a nun as she was receiving food and drink.
> Approaching her, I said, "Make me go forth to
> homelessness."
>
> And she was sympathetic to me and Patachara made
> me go forth,
> she gave me advice and pointed me toward the highest
> goal.
>
> I listened to her words and I put into action her advice.
> That excellent woman's advice was not empty,
> I know the three things that most don't know,
> nothing fouls my heart.

We can see in poems like Chanda's not only individual displays of compassion in worlds of injustice, such as how Patachara treats Chanda in her hunger, but also the sensibility about evident wrongness that the world is this way. Apart from the later and more doctrinal-inflected poem of Isidasi, we generally do not see in the *Therīgāthā* any explanations of the social suffering that befalls women and the poor as due to the karmic fruits of previous actions on their part. On the contrary, the poems of the *Therīgāthā* often make us sympathize with the undeserved suffering of women and this quality was surely part of why the *Therīgāthā* had the appeal that it did for modern Indian social reformers, like Rahul Sankrityayan, and for Dalits (formerly, "untouchables") in the twentieth century who were drawn to Buddhism as an alternative vision of society and as well as offering the possibility of individual self-determination despite the oppressive social contexts.[39]

The modern reception of the poems in the *Therīgāthā* encourages us to read these poems not only to learn about the distant past but also because they can speak to us about the present and about the future, sharing with us their news that has stayed news.

Acknowledgments

This work would not be were it not for Sheldon Pollock. The initial idea that a new translation of the *Therīgāthā* should be done was his; in the long period it took for me actually to do it, he was unflagging in his encouragement, constant in his patience, generous in his guidance and suggestions for improvement, and persistent in his commitment to see it all completed. I thank him for all this and much more as well.

This work would also not be were it not for the generosity, instruction, and example of my teacher, the late G. D. Wijayawardhana, who continues to be for me the very model of what a scholar and a *sahṛdaya* of literature should be.

I am grateful to Beatrice Chrystall for her help with the edition of the Pali text found here.

I thank Lilian Handlin for arranging for a copy of the Chatthasangayana edition of the *Therīgāthā* to be sent to me from Burma. I also thank Charles Carstens for his help with some Burmese material and for reading some of the Pali text of the *Therīgāthā* with me, to my benefit.

I am especially grateful to Liyanage Amarakeerthi for his willingness to read with me the work of Martin Wickramasinghe relevant to the appreciation of the *Therīgāthā*. The importance of the work we did together is evident in this introduction and throughout the translation.

I am grateful for the encouragement and enthusiasm of Preeti Chopra; her support was crucial for the completion of this work.

This work is for my wife, Janet Gyatso. It also would not be were it not for her.

NOTES

1 Masefield 1994: 2–3, translation slightly adapted.

2 Pound 1960: 29.

3 The comments in this sentence and the one before closely follow Hardy 1994: 224–225, 227.

4 There is no single method or type of criteria that allows us to date the individual poems of the *Therīgāthā* with certainty, and scholars have tried to use doctrinal, metrical, and linguistic criteria to establish relative dating for individual poems in the anthology. For example, it has been argued that the poems of Isidasi and Sumedha are among the latest in the collection on the basis of their doctrinal contents. Sometimes the various methods used for dating are not only inconclusive but yield results that are contradictory in the details. Still, as Norman says, when all the results are put together, "we may . . . conclude that all the evidence supports the view that the verses collected together in the [*Therīgāthā*] were uttered over a period of about 300 years, from the end of the 6th century to the end of the 3rd century B.C." (Norman 2007: xxxi.) See also von Hinüber 1996: 53; and Lienhard 1975.

5 Neumann and Majumdar both used Pischel's 1883 edition of the *Therīgāthā* for their translations. This pioneering work was published by the Pali Text Society in England, but it is widely seen as an unsatisfactory edition today. (See Norman 2007: xxxvii and Warder 1967: 1.) What the translations of Neumann, Majumdar,

and Caroline Rhys Davids indicate is that even an unsatisfactory edition of the *Therīgāthā* is capable of giving access to key aspects of the text, including its pleasures as literature.

6 Wickramasinghe 1992: 207. The German translation would be Neumann's 1899 translation. The Sinhala word for "delight" that Wickramasinghe uses is *camatkārayak*, a *tatsama* of one of the central terms in Sanskrit literary theory.

7 Wickramasinghe 1992: 222.

8 This is *Guttila kāvyaya*, one the classics of Sinhala literature, which was written in the fifteenth century.

9 Wickramasinghe 1992: 203. Translation by Liyanage Amarakeerthi and Charles Hallisey.

10 Wickramasinghe 1992: 207. Translation by Liyanage Amarakeerthi and Charles Hallisey.

11 Murcott 1991: 130.

12 Eliot, "On Poetry and Poets," quoted in Pollock 1977: 11.

13 See Pollock 1977: 14. It is, of course, quite another issue if it is assumed that the use of meter is to facilitate memorization and the oral transmission of texts, as is still frequently assumed in studies of early Buddhist texts.

14 Warder 1967: 221.

15 Warder 1967: 103.

16 Pound 1960: 14.

17 See Lienhard 1975.

18 See Collins 2000 for an overview of conventional Buddhist perspectives on the body.

19 Wickramasinghe 1992: 208–209. Translation by Liyanage Amarakeerthi and Charles Hallisey.

20 Carter and Palihawadana 2000: xxvi.

21 Horner 1963: xiii–xiv.

22 Horner 1963: xv. The Sarvāstivādins were another school of early Indian Buddhism, associated particularly with northwest India; on their canon, only parts of which survive and most only in their Chinese translations, see Willemen, Dessein, and Cox 1998: 60–92.

23 Collett 2013.

24 See Bodhi 2000: 221–230.

25 These are noted in the endnotes to the edition here.

26 For example, reference to the *Therīgāthā* is absent from the

Saddharmaratnāvaliya, a medieval Sinhala version of the *Dhammapada* commentary which does tell the stories of some of the *therīs* included in the *Therīgāthā;* see Obeyesekere 2001.

27 See Bartholomeusz 1994.

28 Von Hinüber 1996: 53; see also Lienhard 1975.

29 This is clear, for example, in Wickramasinghe's comment that "The Therigatha is poetry that encourages us to make the heart happy by taming the senses. The fact that there was no poet in Sri Lanka who considered the Therigatha to be great poetry shows how the Sinhala people sadly and inevitably lost their own spiritual riches after the eighth century" (Wickramasinghe 1992: 210. Translation by Liyanage Amarakeerthi and Charles Hallisey).

30 Hardy 1994: 221.

31 See vv. 6, 8, and 9.

32 Verse 479.

33 See S V.420; Bodhi 2000: 1843–1852.

34 Verses 43, 69, 103.

35 See Collins 1982 and Hamilton 2000.

36 There is one set of such poems that begins with Patachara and a group of five hundred students of Patachara, all of whom had children die; right after the verses of Patachara's five hundred students is the poem by Vasetthi, another woman had lost a child and further away, there are the poems of Ubbiri and Kisagotami whose children had also died.

37 We see this, for example, with Patachara and her different groups of students. Dhammapala often highlights this in his commentary, mentioning, for example, just how many of the *therīs* were the students of Mahapajapati Gotami, the stepmother of the Buddha, as well as other affective affinities between women, such as being together in the harem of the future Buddha before he renounced or two nuns who each renounced out of the grief felt after the death of a common friend.

38 Wijayaratna 2010: 140–141.

39 This is part of the modern Indian reception of the *Therīgāthā* in Hindi translations, as for example, Upadhyaya 1950.

NOTE ON THE TEXT AND TRANSLATION

The text of the *Therīgāthā* presented here is essentially a transcription of the verses as they are found in the edition of the Dhammapala's commentary on the *Therīgāthā*. This was prepared by Bihalpola Siri Dewarakkhita Thera, revised by Mahagoda Siri Nanissara Thera, and published in Sinhala script in the Simon Hewavitarne Bequest Series in 1918. For the text here, the verses were extracted from the commentary and then numbered on the model of what is found in other editions of the canonical *Therīgāthā*.[1] Also added to the text are the rubrics that name the divisions (*nipāta*) of poems based on length; these rubrics are found in the canonical *Therīgāthā* and in Dhammapala's commentary.

Since the publication of Richard Pischel's *editio princeps* in 1883, scholars have recognized the need to establish critically a better text of the *Therīgāthā*. While there have been many important contributions toward addressing this need over the years, these studies have also made it very clear just how difficult the task of critically editing the *Therīgāthā* in a satisfactory and responsible way will be. It remains a task for the future.

A number of authoritative editions have been published in the countries where Theravada Buddhism is found and they often contain better readings of the *Therīgāthā* verses than Pischel had available to him.[2] These improved readings have been central to the scholarly efforts to establish a better text of the *Therīgāthā*.[3] The 1918 Sri Lankan edition of the commentary to the *Therīgāthā*, presented here, is one of the most important of these, as can be seen especially by the frequent recourse to it in the valuable text-critical work by K. R. Norman that is found in the notes to his translation of the *Therīgāthā*; equally important in this regard is the Burmese edition of the text that was prepared as part of the Sixth Council (Chatthasangayana) in Rangoon.

Both the Sri Lankan and Burmese editions make it clear that the Pali in their texts has been subjected to both simplification and normalization as part of the efforts of the editors, all learned Buddhist monks, to present a lucid and readable text. This obviously reduces some of their value as aids for restoring the text of the *Therīgāthā* to the earliest form possible, but these same features commend themselves to readers looking for reliable, readable, and representative presentations of the text. Indeed, the text established by Bihalpola Siri Dewarakkhita Thera and Mahagoda Siri Nanissara Thera is lucid and authoritative, representing as it does the reception tradition for the text in Sri Lanka. It should be emphasized that the text presented here is not meant to provide the many variant readings extant for the *Therīgāthā*—even the variant readings provided in the critical apparatus of the Bihalpola and Mahagoda edition are not included here—let alone to be a critical edition. Those readers who are interested in pursuing such text-critical questions should consult K. R. Norman's translation of the *Therīgāthā* for references to relevant editions and scholarly work as well as for Norman's own discussions of possible textual restorations and emendations that are found in his very important notes to individual verses. The notes to individual verses in Norman's translation remain essential resources for all scholarship on the *Therīgāthā*, and indeed, for reading the work in Pali.

It is clear from Dhammapala's commentary that the text of the *Therīgāthā* he had in front of him was already filled with problems. Dhammapala's efforts to deal with these textual difficulties have been helpful to scholars from Pischel on,[4] in their efforts to establish the text of the *Therīgāthā*, just as more generally, Dhammapala's interpretation of the verses is invaluable for anyone who wants to read the *Therīgāthā*.[5]

I have generally followed Dhammapala's understanding of individual verses in my translations. This is not to say that Dhammapala was not sometimes wrong in his interpretations, as has been pointed out in modern scholarship (see, in particular Wright 1999), but in general when Dhammapala's interpretation of a verse has been textually plausible, I have chosen to follow his lead. Some of the poems in the *Therīgāthā* are dialogues, and I have also followed Dhammapala in identifying the different voices and have included his identifications in the translations themselves. It should also be noted that in some cases I have made explicit in the English what is obvious but only implicit in the Pali. This is especially the case in those poems where there is a pun on the *therī's* name, and the verse indicates that the name a *therī* has is literally appropriate for her, as for example, in the first line of verse 7, in which Vira repeats what the Buddha had said to her:

vīrā vīrehi dhammehi bhikkhunī bhāvitindriyā

The name you are called by means hero, Vira,

it's a good name for you because of your heroic
qualities,
you are a nun who knows how to know well...

The first line of the translation, kept separate from the rest, is meant to display the significance of the opening vocative, "Vira." It is worth noting here that one of the peculiar features of the *Therīgāthā* is the extensive use of vocatives in the poems, often the *therī* addressing herself, but thus also identifying herself as the author of the poem.[6]

Dhammapala's commentary on the *Therīgāthā* is an elaborate and sophisticated work. In addition to glosses on individual words and interpretations of individual poems, Dhammapala also provides background information on the individual authors of the poems and the circumstances of the composition of the poem. Summaries of what Dhammapala says about the authors in their present are provided in the first endnote to each poem; Dhammapala also often gives stories about the past lives of the *therīs* which help us to understand, in Dhammapala's eyes, why the individual women were ready for the spiritual achievements they attained in their present lives. In the course of providing background information on each *therī,* Dhammapala also quotes from the canonical *Apadāna,* which is found in the same section of the Pali canon as the *Therīgāthā*. Dhammapala's commentary on the *Therīgāthā,* the *Paramatthadīpanī,* has been translated by William Pruitt and that translation is an excellent companion for reading the *Therīgāthā*; the summaries of the *therīs'* lives in the notes are based on this translation.[7]

NOTES

1 There is not, however, consensus on the number of verses in the *Therīgāthā*. In P, there are 522; in C, 524; and in Sri Dharmakirti Dhammananda's 1926 edition, there are 525. In H, there are actually 527 *gāthās*, and the difference in number from the text presented here is because of a difference in verse division. Some of the manuscripts used by Pischel have an addendum that says that there are 494 verses (see P 174); see also von Hinüber 1996: 51–52.

2 Norman 2007: xxxvii.

3 Wright 1999, however, rightly commends the value of a probative attitude toward Dhammapala's understandings of the *Therīgāthā* especially for establishing the text of the *Therīgāthā*.

4 Pischel says, "Indeed, without the commentary I should hardly have ventured to publish this text at all" (Pischel 1966: 120).

5 Norman, for example, observes, "As a general rule, I have tried to recover and translate the text which Dhammapala commented on, if this seemed to be metrical and to make sense or any [variant readings] which Dhammapala quoted" (Norman 2007: xxxvi).

6 See von Hinüber 1996: 52.

7 Pruitt 1999.

THERIGATHA

ekakanipāto

therikā

1 sukhaṃ supāhi therike katvā coḷena pārutā
upasanto hi te rāgo sukkhaḍākaṃ va kumbhiyaṃ ti.

muttā

2 mutte muccassu yogehi cando rāhuggahā iva
vippamuttena cittena anaṇā bhuñja piṇḍākan ti.

POEMS WITH ONE VERSE

Therika

Spoken by the Buddha to her

Now[1] that you live among *therīs*, Therika, 1
the name you were given as a child finally becomes you.

So sleep well, covered with cloth you have made,
your passion for sex shriveled away
like a herb dried up in a pot.

Mutta

Spoken by the Buddha to her

The[2] name you are called by means freed, Mutta, 2

so be freed from what holds you back,
like the moon from the grasp of Rahu[3]
at the end of an eclipse.
When nothing is owed because the mind is completely free
you can relish food collected as alms.

puṇṇā

3 puṇṇe pūrassu dhammehi cando pannarasoriva
paripuṇṇāya paññāya tamokkhandhaṃ padālayā ti.

tissā

4 tisse sikkhassu sikkhāya mā tam yogā upaccaguṃ
sabbayogavisaṃyuttā cara loke anāsavā ti.

aññatarā tissā

5 tisse yuñjassu dhammehi khaṇo taṃ mā upaccagā
khaṇātītā hi socanti nirayamhi samappitā ti.

Punna

Spoken by the Buddha to her

The[4] name you are called by means full, Punna, 3

so be filled with good things, like the moon when it is full,
break through all that is dark with wisdom made full.

Tissa

Spoken by the Buddha to her

Tissa,[5] train yourself strictly, don't let 4
what can hold you back overwhelm you.
When you are free from everything that holds you back
you can live in the world
without the depravities that ooze out from within.

Another Tissa

Addressing herself, repeating what was spoken by the Buddha to her

Tissa,[6] hold fast to good things, don't let the moment 5
    escape.
Those who end up in hell cry over moments now past.

dhīrā

6 dhīre nirodhaṃ phussehi saññāvūpasamaṃ sukhaṃ
ārādhayāhi nibbānaṃ yogakkhemaṃ anuttaraṃ ti.[1]

vīrā

7 vīrā vīrehi dhammehi bhikkhunī bhāvitindriyā
dhārehi antimaṃ dehaṃ chetvā māraṃ savāhanaṃ ti.

Dhira

Addressing herself, repeating what was spoken by the Buddha to her

The name you are called by means self-reliance, Dhira, 6

so know these for yourself:
cessation, the stilling of projections, happiness.
Attain nibbana, unsurpassed safety from all that holds you back.[7]

Vira

Addressing herself, repeating what was spoken by the Buddha to her

The name you are called by means hero, Vira, 7

it's a good name for you because of your heroic qualities,
you are a nun who knows how to know well.[8]
Take care of the body, it's your last,
just make sure it doesn't become a vehicle for death after this.

mittā

8 saddhāya pabbajitvāna mitte mittaratā bhava
bhāvehi kusale dhamme yogakkhemassa pattiyā ti.

bhadrā

9 saddhāya pabbajitvāna bhadre bhadraratā bhava
bhāvehi kusale dhamme yogakkhemaṃ anuttaraṃ ti.

Mitta

Addressing herself, repeating what was spoken by the Buddha to her

The name you are called by means friend, Mitta, 8

you became a nun out of faith,
now be someone who delights in friends,
become morally skillful
for the sake of that unsurpassed safety from all that holds you back.

Bhadra

Addressing herself, repeating what was spoken by the Buddha to her

The name you are called by means auspicious, Bhadra, 9

you became a nun out of faith,
now be someone who delights in auspicious things,
become morally skillful
for the sake of that unsurpassed safety from all that holds you back.

upasamā

10 upasame tare oghaṃ maccudheyyaṃ suduttaraṃ
dhārehi antimaṃ dehaṃ chetvā māraṃ savāhanaṃ ti.

muttā

11 sumuttā sādhumuttamhi tīhi khujjehi muttiyā
udukkhalena musalena patinā khujjakena ca
muttamhi jātimaraṇā bhavanetti samūhatā ti.

Upasama

Addressing herself, repeating what was spoken by the Buddha to her

The name you are called by means calm, Upasama, 10

you should cross the flood where death holds sway,
hard as it is to cross.
Take care of the body, it's your last,
but make sure it doesn't become a vehicle for death after
this.

Mutta

The[9] name I am called by means freed 11

and I am quite free, well-free from three crooked things,
mortar, pestle, and husband with his own crooked thing.
I am freed from birth and death,
what leads to rebirth has been rooted out.

dhammadinnā

12 chandajātā avasāyī manasā ca phuṭhā siyā
kāmesu appaṭibaddhacittā uddhaṃsotā vimuccatī[2] ti

visākhā

13 karotha buddhasāsanaṃ yaṃ katvā nānutappati
khippaṃ pādāni dhovitvā ekamante nisīdathā ti.[3]

sumanā

14 dhātuyo dukkhato disvā mā jātiṃ punarāgami
bhave chandaṃ virājetvā upasantā carissasī ti.

Dhammadinna

She[10] who has given rise to the wish for freedom 12
and is set on it, shall be clear in mind.
One whose heart is not caught in the pleasures of the senses,
one who is bound upstream,[11] will be freed.

Visakha

Do[12] what the Buddha taught, 13
there's nothing to be sorry about after doing it.
Quick, wash the feet, sit down off to one side.

Sumana

Once[13] you see as suffering 14
even the basic bits that make up everything,[14]
you won't be born again,
calm is how you will live
once you discard the desire for more lives.

uttarā

15 kāyena saṃvutā āsiṃ vācāya uda cetasā
samūlaṃ taṇhaṃ abbuyha sītibhūtamhi nibbutā ti.

vuḍḍhapabbajitasumanā

16 sukhaṃ tvaṃ vuḍḍhike sehi katvā coḷena pārūtā
upasanto hi te rāgo sītibhūtāsi nibbutā ti.

dhammā

17 piṇḍapātaṃ caritvāna daṇḍam olubbha dubbalā
vedhamānehi gattehi tattheva nipatiṃ chamā
disvā ādīnavaṃ kāye atha cittaṃ vimucci me ti.

Uttara

Self-controlled[15] with the body, 15
with speech, and with the mind,
having pulled out craving down to the root,
I have become cool, free.

Sumana who renounced in old age

Addressing herself

Sleep[16] well, dear old one, 16
covered with cloth you have made,
your passion for sex has shriveled away,
you've become cool, free.

Dhamma

Wandering[17] about for alms, 17
but weak, leaning on a stick with limbs shaking,
I fell to the ground right there,
and seeing the danger in the body, my heart was freed.

saṅghā

18 hitvā ghare pabbajitā hitvā puttaṃ pasuṃ piyaṃ
hitvā rāgañ ca dosañ ca avijjañ ca virājiya
samūlaṃ taṇham abbuyha upasantamhi nibbutā[4] ti.

Sangha

Abandoning[18] houses, going forth, 18
giving up son,[19] livestock, and all that is dear,
leaving behind desire, anger, and ignorance,
discarding them all,
having pulled out craving down to the root,
I have become cool, I am free.

dukanipāto

abhirūpanandā

19 āturaṃ asuciṃ pūtiṃ passa nande samussayaṃ
asubhāya cittaṃ bhāvehi ekaggaṃ susamāhitaṃ.[1]

20 animittaṃ ca bhāvehi mānānusayam ujjaha
tato mānābhisamayā upasantā carissasī ti.

jentā[2]

21 ye ime sattabojjhaṅgā maggā nibbānapattiyā
bhāvitā te mayā sabbe yathā buddhena desitā.[3]

22 diṭṭho hi me so bhagavā antimo yaṃ samussayo
vikkhīṇo jātisaṃsāro natthi dāni punabbhavo ti.

POEMS WITH TWO VERSES

Abhirupananda

Spoken by the Buddha to her as instruction

Your[1] name means delighting in beauty, Nanda, 19

Look at this body, Nanda, it's sick, it's dirty, it's foul.

Use what is unpleasant to cultivate the mind,
make it focused and attentive.

Cultivate open mindfulness, let go of predispositions, 20
by mastery over conceit, calm is how you will live.

Jenta

I[2] have cultivated all seven wings of awakening,[3] 21
paths to the attainment of nibbana
just as they were taught by the Buddha.

I have seen the lord, 22
this is the last body, the swirl of rebirth finally finished,
there is no more birth ahead.

sumaṅgalamātā

23 sumuttike sumuttike sādhu muttikamhi musalassa
ahiriko me chattakaṃ vāpi ukkhalikā me deḍḍubhaṃ vāti.

24 rāgañ ca ahaṃ dosañ ca cicciṭi cicciṭīti vihanāmi
sā rukkhamūlaṃ upagamma aho sukhanti sukhato
jhāyāmī ti.

Sumangala's Mother

Addressing her son

Dear[4] one who is quite free, dear one who is quite freed, 23
I too am well-freed from the pestle;
my shameless husband, even the sunshade he worked
under,
and my pot that stinks like a water snake all disgust me.

As I destroyed anger and the passion for sex, 24
I was reminded of the sound of bamboo being split,
I go to the foot of a tree and think, "Ah, happiness,"
and from within that happiness, I begin to meditate.

aḍḍhakāsī

25 yāva kāsijanapado suṅko me tatthako ahū
tam katvā negamo aggham aḍḍhenaggham ṭhapesi mam.

26 atha nibbindaham rūpe nibbindañ ca virajjaham
mā puna jātisaṃsāraṃ sandhāveyyaṃ punappunaṃ
tisso vijjā sacchikatā kataṃ buddhassa sāsanan ti.

Addhakasi

There[5] is a reason why I was called "Half-Kasi."[6] 25

As much as the country of Kasi was worth,
my price was just the same;
while that was once my value,
after too many customers
my worth was cut by half.

By then I had enough 26
of what my body brought
and wearied I turned away.
May I not be reborn again and again
in endless and inevitable births.
I have seen with my own eyes
the three things that most don't know,[7]
what the Buddha taught is done.

cittā

27 kiñcāpi khomhi kisikā gilānā bāḷhadubbalā
daṇḍam olubbha gacchāmi pabbataṃ abhirūhiya.

28 saṅghāṭiṃ nikkhipitvāna pattakaṃ ca nikujjiya
sele khambhesim attānaṃ tamokkhandhaṃ padāliyā ti.

mettikā

29 kiñcāpi khomhi dukkhitā dubbalā gatayobbanā
daṇḍam olubbha gacchāmi pabbataṃ abhirūhiya.

30 nikkhipitvāna saṅghāṭiṃ pattakaṃ ca nikujjiya
nisinnā camhi selamhi atha cittaṃ vimucci me
tisso vijjā anuppattā kataṃ buddhassa sāsanan ti.

Chitta

Even[8] though I am emaciated, exhausted, and very weak, 27
still I go on, leaning on a stick, climbing the mountain.

I have thrown off my outer robe 28
turned my bowl over,
I leaned against a rock
after splitting open
the mass of mental darkness.

Mettika

Even[9] though I am suffering, weak, my youth gone, 29
still I go on, leaning on a stick, climbing the mountain.

I threw off my outer robe and turned my bowl over, 30
I sit on a rock, my heart is freed,
the three things that most don't know[10] are mine,
what the Buddha taught is done.

mittā

31 cātuddasiṃ pañcadasiṃ yā ca pakkhassa aṭṭhamī
pāṭihāriyapakkhañ ca aṭṭhaṅgasusamāgataṃ
uposathaṃ upāgañchiṃ devakāyābhinandinī

32 sājja ekena bhattena muṇḍā saṅghāṭipārutā
devakāyaṃ na pattheham vineyya hadaye daran ti.

abhayamātu

33 uddhaṃ pādatalā amma adho ve kesamatthakā
paccavekkhassumaṃ kāyaṃ asuciṃ pūtigandhikaṃ.

34 evaṃ viharamānāya sabbo rāgo samūhato
pariḷāho samucchinno sītibhūtamhi nibbutā ti.

Mitta

Usually[11] people do all eight lay precepts 31
only on an Uposatha[12] day,
but I did them on the fourteenth, fifteenth, eighth,
and even on other days of every fortnight,
happy that a god's body would be mine one day.

Today I eat just one meal a day, 32
my head is shaved,
and wear the outer robe of a nun.
My heart's fear and its sorrow are gone:
I don't want a god's body either.

Abhaya's Mother

Addressing herself, first repeating what was spoken to her by her son

"Whether[13] up from the sole of the foot, Mother, 33
or down from the top of the head,
reflect on this body as filthy and foul-smelling."

It's by living that way that all passion for sex is pulled out. 34
Its burning fever broken, I have become cool, free.

abhayā

35 abhaye bhiduro kāyo yattha sattā puthujjanā
nikkhipissāmimaṃ dehaṃ sampajānā satīmatī.

36 bahūhi dukkhadhammehi appamādaratāya me
taṇhakkhayo anuppatto kataṃ buddhassa sāsanan ti.

sāmā

37 catukkhattuṃ pañcakkhattuṃ vihārā upanikkhamiṃ
aladdhā cetaso santiṃ citte avasavattini.[4]

38 tassā me aṭṭhamī ratti yato taṇhā samūhatā
bahūhi dukkhadhammehi appamādaratāya me
taṇhakkhayo anuppatto kataṃ buddhassa sāsanan ti.

Abhaya

Beginning with words that the Buddha spoke to her

"Abhaya,[14] ordinary people cling to this fragile body," 35
he said, and told me to be attentive and mindful,
that I should discard this body.

I have achieved the end of craving, 36
because of a delight in diligence,
a delight that was prompted
by the many things that are nothing but suffering.
What the Buddha taught is done.

Sama

Four[15] times, five times, I went out from the monastery, 37
with no peace in my heart, no control over my mind.

But this is the eighth night since I rooted out craving, 38
I have achieved the end of craving,
and what the Buddha taught is done
because of a delight in diligence
a delight that was prompted
by the many things that are nothing but suffering.

tikanipāto

aparā sāmā

39 paṇṇavīsativassāni yato pabbajitāya me
nābhijānāmi cittassa samaṃ laddhaṃ kudācanaṃ.

40 aladdhā cetaso santiṃ citte avasavattini[1]
tato saṃvegam āpādiṃ saritvā jinasāsanaṃ.

41 bahūhi dukkhadhammehi appamādaratāya me
taṇhakkhayo anuppatto kataṃ buddhassa sāsanaṃ
ajja me sattamī ratti yato taṇhā visositā ti.

POEMS WITH THREE VERSES

Another Sama

My[1] name may mean one who has peace of mind, 39

but I am not aware of ever having had any peace of mind,
even though it has been twenty-five years since I went
forth.

No peace of heart, no control over my mind, 40
I began to fear the inevitable,
after remembering the teaching of the Conqueror.[2]

The end of craving has been achieved by me 41
and what the Buddha taught is done
because of delight in diligence
prompted by the many things that are nothing but
suffering.

Today is the seventh night since craving was destroyed
for me.

uttamā

42 catukkhattuṃ pañcakkhattuṃ vihārā upanikkhamiṃ
aladdhā cetaso santiṃ citte avasavattinī.[2]

43 sā bhikkhuniṃ upagacchiṃ yā me saddhāyikā ahu
sā me dhammam adesesi khandhāyatanadhātuyo.[3]

44 tassā dhammaṃ suṇitvāna yathā maṃ anusāsi sā
sattāhaṃ ekapallaṅkena nisīdiṃ pītisukhasamappitā
aṭṭhamiyā pāde pasāresiṃ tamokkhandhaṃ padāliyā ti.

Uttama

Four[3] times, five times, I went out from the monastery, 42
heart without peace, heart out of control.

I approached the nun, 43
she seemed like someone I could trust.
She taught me the dhamma
about what makes a person
about the senses and their objects
and about the basic elements that make up everything.[4]

I listened to what she taught, 44
did exactly as she said,
for seven days I sat in one position, legs crossed,
given over to joy and happiness.
On the eighth day I stretched out my feet,
after splitting open the mass of mental darkness.

aparā uttamā

45 ye ime sattabojjhaṅgā maggā nibbānapattiyā
bhāvitā te mayā sabbe yathā buddhena desitā.[4]

46 suññatassānimittassa lābhinīhaṃ yadicchakaṃ
orasā dhītā buddhassa nibbānābhiratā sadā.

47 sabbe kāmā samucchinnā ye dibbā ye ca mānusā
vikkhīṇo jātisaṃsāro natthi dāni punabbhavo ti.

Another Uttama

I have cultivated all seven wings of awakening, 45
paths to the attainment of nibbana
just as they were taught by the Buddha.

I enjoy whenever I want 46
that which is empty, without mark or measure,[5]
I am a true daughter of the Buddha,
always delighting in nibbana.

The urge for all sensual pleasures is cut off, 47
whether they be heavenly or human,
the swirl of rebirth is completely finished,
now there is no more birth ahead.

dantikā

48 divā vihārā nikkhamma gijjhakūṭamhi pabbate
nāgam ogāhamuttiṇṇaṃ nadītīramhi addasaṃ.

49 puriso aṅkusam ādāya dehi pādanti yācati
nāgo pasārayī pādaṃ puriso nāgam āruhi.

50 disvā adantaṃ damitaṃ manussā naṃ vasaṃ gataṃ
tato cittaṃ samādhesiṃ khalu tāya vanaṃ gatā ti.

Dantika

Having[6] come out 48
from where I had spent the day on Mount Gijjhakuta,
I saw an elephant on the riverbank that had come out
from the river it had plunged into.

A man holding a goad told the elephant, "Hold up your foot." 49
and the elephant put its foot forward and the man climbed on.

I saw how the untamed was tamed, 50
how the animal was ruled by the human.
I concentrated my mind,
I went to the forest just for that.

ubbiri

51 amma jīvā ti vanamhi kandasi attānaṃ adhigaccha ubbiri
cullāsītisahassāni sabbā jīvasanāmikā
etamhāḷāhane daḍḍhā tāsaṃ kam anusocasi.

52 abbahī vata me sallaṃ duddasaṃ hadayassitaṃ
yaṃ me sokaparetāya dhītusokaṃ vyapānudi.

53 sājja abbūḷhasallāhaṃ nicchātā parinibbutā
buddhaṃ dhammañ ca saṅghañ ca upemi saraṇaṃ
munin ti.

Ubbiri

Spoken by the Buddha to her

Mother,[7] you cry in the forest, "O Jiva,"[8] 51
get hold of yourself, Ubbiri.
Eighty-four thousand daughters, all with that same name,
the ones that said they were "Life,"
all have been burnt in this cremation ground,
so which one of them are you grieving for?

Spoken by Ubbiri

He pulled out the arrow that was hard for me to see, 52
the one that I nourished in my heart,
he expelled the grief for a daughter,
the grief that had overwhelmed me.

Today the arrow is pulled out, 53
I am without hunger, completely free.
I go to the Buddha, his dhamma, and his sangha[9] for
refuge,
I go to the Sage for refuge.

sukkā

54 kiṃ me katā rājagahe manussā madhupītā va acchare
ye sukkaṃ na upāsanti desentiṃ buddhasāsanaṃ.

55 tañ ca appaṭivānīyaṃ asecanakam ojavaṃ
pivanti maññe sappaññā valāhakam ivaddhagū.

56 sukkā sukkehi dhammehi vītarāgā samāhitā
dhāreti antimaṃ dehaṃ jetvā māraṃ savāhanan ti.[5]

Sukka

Spoken by a deity about her

What[10] has happened to these men of Rajagaha? 54
They sit like they are drunk,
they do not sit near Sukka
as she teaches what the Buddha taught.

I think those with wisdom drink something else, 55
something that gives strength, is delicious and irresistible,
they drink like travelers who gulp rain
just fallen from a dark cloud.

Spoken by Sukka

The name you are called by means bright, Sukka 56
it's a good name for you because of your bright mental
states.
Take care of the body, it's your last,
just make sure it doesn't become a vehicle for death after
this.

selā

57 natthi nissaraṇaṃ loke kiṃ vivekena kāhasi
bhuñjāhi kāmaratiyo māhu pacchānutāpinī.[6]

58 sattisūlūpamā kāmā khandhāsaṃ adhikuṭṭanā
yaṃ tvaṃ kāmaratiṃ brūsi aratī dāni sā mama.[7]

59 sabbattha vihatā nandī tamokkhandho padālito
evaṃ jānāhi pāpima nihato tvam asi antakā ti.[8]

Sela

Spoken by Mara to her

There[11] is no freedom in the world, 57
what will you accomplish by being all alone?
Enjoy the pleasures of sex now,
you won't regret it later.

Sela replied

The pleasures of sex are like swords and stakes, 58
the body, senses, and the mind
just the chopping block on which they cut.
What you call the delights of sexual pleasure
are no delights for me now.

What you take as pleasures are not for me, 59
the mass of mental darkness is split open.
Know this, evil one, you are defeated, you are finished.

somā

60 yaṃ taṃ isīhi pattabbaṃ ṭhānaṃ durabhisambhavaṃ
na taṃ dvaṅgulapaññāya sakkā pappotum itthiyā.

61 itthibhāvo no kiṃ kayirā cittamhi susamāhite
ñāṇamhi vattamānamhi sammā dhammaṃ vipassato.[9]

62 sabbattha vihatā nandī tamokkhandho padālito
evaṃ jānāhi pāpima nihato tvam asi antakā ti.[10]

Soma

Spoken by Mara to her

It[12] is hard to get to the place that sages want to reach, 60
it's not possible for a woman,
especially not one with only two fingers' worth of wisdom.

Soma replied

What does being a woman have to do with it? 61
What counts is that the heart is settled
and that one sees what really is.

What you take as pleasures are not for me, 62
the mass of mental darkness is split open.
Know this, evil one, you are defeated, you are finished.

catukkanipāto

bhaddā kāpilānī

63 putto buddhassa dāyādo kassapo susamāhito
pubbenivāsaṃ yo vedi saggāpāyañ ca passati.

64 atho jātikkhayaṃ patto abhiññāvosito muni
etāhi tīhi vijjāhi tevijjo hoti brāhmaṇo.

65 tatheva bhaddā kāpilānī tevijjā maccuhāyinī
dhāreti antimaṃ dehaṃ jetvā māraṃ savāhanaṃ.[1]

66 disvā ādīnavaṃ loke ubho pabbajitā mayaṃ
tyamha khīṇāsavā dantā sītibhūtamha nibbutā ti.

A POEM WITH FOUR VERSES

Bhadda Kapilani

Kassapa[1] is an heir of the Buddha, his son, well-settled in heart. 63
He knows his previous lives, he sees heaven and hell.

He has ended rebirth, perfected higher knowledge, 64
he is a sage, he has become a real Brahman
because he knows the three things that most don't know.[2]

In exactly the same way, Bhadda Kapilani 65
knows the three things that most don't know,
she has left death behind,
she takes care of the body, knowing it's her last,
making sure it doesn't become a vehicle for death after this.

Once we were husband and wife, 66
but seeing the danger in the world, we both went forth,
we removed our defiling compulsions,
we became cool, free.

pañcakanipāto

aññatarā

67 paṇṇavīsativassāni yato pabbajitā ahaṃ
nāccharāsaṅghātamattam pi cittassūpasamajjhagaṃ.

68 aladdhā cetaso santiṃ kāmarāgenavassutā
bāhā paggayha kandantī vihāraṃ pāvisiṃ ahaṃ.

69 sā bhikkhuniṃ upāgacchiṃ yā me saddhāyikā ahu
sā me dhammam adesesi khandhāyatanadhātuyo.[1]

70 tassā dhammaṃ suṇitvāna ekamante upāvisiṃ
pubbenivāsaṃ jānāmi dibbacakkhu visodhitaṃ.

71 ceto pariccañāṇañ ca sotadhātu visodhitā
iddhī pi me sacchikatā patto me āsavakkhayo
chaḷabhiññā sacchikatā kataṃ buddhassa sāsanan ti.[2]

freedom seems to be the goal

POEMS WITH FIVE VERSES

The verses of a certain nun

It's[1] been twenty-five years since I renounced 67
but not for a moment, not even a finger's snap,
did I experience stilling of my mind.

With no peace in my heart, dripping with sexual desire, 68
I entered the monastery, wailing, my arms outstretched.

I approached the nun, 69
she seemed like someone I could trust.
She taught me the dhamma
about what makes a person
about the senses and their objects
and about the basic elements that make up everything.[2]

Hearing the dhamma from her, I came to her side, 70
I know my previous lives,
and the eye that can see the invisible is clear.

I know the ways of my heart, now I hear clearly. 71
Powers beyond normal are known at first hand,
the depravities that ooze out from within are wasted away,
the six powers[3] attained, the teaching of the Buddha
is done.

vimalā

72 mattā vaṇṇena rūpena sobhaggena yasena ca
yobbanena cupatthaddhā aññāsamatimaññihaṃ.

73 vibhūsitvā imaṃ kāyaṃ sucittaṃ bālalāpanaṃ
aṭṭhāsiṃ vesidvāramhi luddo pāsam ivoḍḍiya.

74 pilandhanaṃ vidaṃsentī guyhaṃ pakāsikaṃ bahuṃ
akāsiṃ vividhaṃ māyaṃ ujjagghantī bahuṃ janaṃ.

75 sājja piṇḍaṃ caritvāna muṇḍā saṅghāṭipārutā
nisinnā rukkhamūlamhi avitakkassa lābhinī.

76 sabbe yogā samucchinnā ye dibbā ye ca mānusā
khepetvā āsave sabbe sītibhūtamhi nibbutā ti.

Vimala

Intoxicated[4] by my good looks, 72
by my body, my beauty, and my reputation,
haughty because of my youth, I looked down on other
women.

I decorated this body, decked out it made fools mutter, 73
a prostitute at the door, like a hunter spreading out the
snare.

I flashed my ornaments as if I was showing my hidden 74
parts,
I created illusions for people, all the while sneering at
them.

↳ like she had the power all along

Today I collected alms, 75
head shaved, covered with the outer robe,
now seated at the foot of the tree.
what I get has nothing to do with schemes. → maturity?

All ties are cut, whether divine or human, 76
I have thrown away all that fouls the heart,
I have become cool, free. → even in the previous poem
↳ what could this mean?

sīhā

77 ayoniso manasikārā kāmarāgena aṭṭitā
ahosiṃ uddhatā pubbe citte avasavattinī.

78 pariyuṭṭhitā kilesehi subhasaññānuvattinī
samaṃ cittassa na labhiṃ rāgacittavasānugā.

79 kisā paṇḍu vivaṇṇā ca satta vassāni cārihaṃ
nāhaṃ divā vā rattiṃ vā sukhaṃ vindiṃ sudukkhitā.

80 tato rajjuṃ gahetvāna pāvisiṃ vanamantaraṃ
varaṃ me idha ubbandhaṃ yañ ca hīnaṃ punācare.

81 daḷhaṃ pāsaṃ karitvāna rukkhasākhāya bandhiya
pakkhipiṃ pāsaṃ gīvāyaṃ atha cittaṃ vimucci me ti.

Siha

Pained[5] by distracted attention and by desire for sex 77
I was always disturbed, without any control over my
thoughts.

Acting on thoughts of happiness, 78
overcome by defiling compulsions,[6]
I had no peace of mind,
controlled by a mind bent on excitement.

Thin, pallid, and wan, I wandered for seven years 79
I did not experience happiness by day or by night,
intense suffering was what I had.

Taking a rope, I went to the forest, thinking 80
"It is better to hang than to live this low life."

I made the noose strong and tied it to a branch, 81
but just as I looped it around my neck, my mind was set
free.

sundarīnandā

82 āturaṃ asuciṃ pūtiṃ passa nande samussayaṃ
asubhāya cittaṃ bhāvehi ekaggaṃ susamāhitaṃ.[3]

83 yathā idaṃ tathā etaṃ yathā etaṃ tathā idaṃ
duggandhaṃ pūtikaṃ vāti bālānaṃ abhinanditaṃ.

84 evam etaṃ avekkhantī rattindivam atanditā
tato sakāya paññāya abhinibbijja dakkhisaṃ.

85 tassā me appamattāya vicinantiyā yoniso
yathā bhūtaṃ ayaṃ kāyo diṭṭho santarabāhiro.

86 atha nibbindihaṃ kāye ajjhattañ ca virajjahaṃ
appamattā visaṃyuttā upasantamhi nibbutā ti.

Sundarinanda

Spoken by the Buddha to her

Look[7] at this body, Nanda, it's sick, it's dirty, it's foul. 82

Use what is unpleasant to cultivate the mind,
make it focused and attentive.

Just as this is, so is that, just as that is, so is this: 83
stinking, foul, the delight of fools.

When you look at it this way, 84
day and night, always intently,
someday you will see,
breaking through with your own wisdom.

Spoken by Sundarinanda

This body was seen as it really is, inside and out, 85
as I examined it carefully and thoroughly.

I became tired of the body, inwardly disinterested, 86
diligent, released, at peace, free.

nanduttarā

87 aggiṃ candañ ca sūriyañ ca devatā ca namassihaṃ
nadītitthāni gantvāna udakaṃ oruhāmihaṃ.

88 bahūvatasamādānā aḍḍhaṃ sīsassa olikhiṃ
chamāya seyyaṃ kappemi rattiṃ bhattaṃ na bhuñjahaṃ.

89 vibhūsā maṇḍanaratā nhāpanucchādanehi ca
upakāsiṃ imaṃ kāyaṃ kāmarāgena aṭṭitā.

90 tato saddhaṃ labhitvāna pabbajiṃ anagāriyaṃ
disvā kāyaṃ yathābhūtaṃ kāmarāgo samūhato.

91 sabbe bhavā samucchinnā icchā ca patthanāpi ca
sabbayogavisaṃyuttā santiṃ pāpuṇi cetaso ti.

Nanduttara

I[8] honored fire, the moon and sun, and gods, 87
at the ford in the river, I went down into the water.

Undertaking many vows, I shaved half my head, 88
I made a bed on the ground, I didn't enjoy food at night.

Vexed as I was by the urge for sex, 89
I would do this body a favor
with baths and massages,
and delight in jewelry and finery.

Then confident, I went forth to homelessness. 90
Once I saw the body as it was, the urge for sex was no
more.

All existences are cut off, wants and aspirations too, 91
every tie untied, I have attained peace of mind.

mittākāḷī

92 saddhāya pabbajitvāna agārasmānagāriyaṃ
vicariṃhaṃ tena tena lābhasakkāraussukā.

93 riñcitvā paramaṃ atthaṃ hīnaṃ attham asevihaṃ
kilesānaṃ vasaṃ gantvā sāmaññatthaṃ na bujjhihaṃ.

94 tassā me ahu saṃvego nisinnāya vihārake
ummaggapaṭipannāmhi taṇhāya vasam āgatā.

95 appakaṃ jīvitaṃ mayhaṃ jarā vyādhi ca maddati
jarāya bhijjati kāyo na me kālo pamajjituṃ.

96 yathābhūtaṃ avekkhantī khandhānaṃ udayabbayaṃ
vimuttacittā uṭṭhāsiṃ kataṃ buddhassa sāsanan ti.

Mittakali

doing the right things for the wrong reasons

I[9] went forth in confidence from home to homelessness, 92
I wandered about, looking for gain and recognition.

I ignored the highest goal, taking to any low goal instead, 93
ruled by defiling compulsions, I never knew what an
ascetic's goal was.

Then while I was seated in my hut I began to fear the 94
inevitable,
I knew I was on the wrong road, under the rule of craving.

Life is short, 95
old age and illness already crush me,
there's no time to waste
before this body is broken by old age.

Looking at a person and 96
seeing that a person is made only of impersonal parts,[10]
seeing those as they changed over time,
waxing and waning,
I stood up, my mind freed,
the Buddha's teaching done.

sakulā

97 agārasmiṃ vasantīhaṃ dhammaṃ sutvāna bhikkhuno
addasaṃ virajaṃ dhammaṃ nibbānaṃ padam accutaṃ.

98 sāhaṃ puttañ ca dhītarañ ca dhanadhaññañ ca chaḍḍiya
kese chedāpayitvāna pabbajiṃ anagāriyaṃ.

99 sikkhamānā ahaṃ santī bhāventī maggam añjasaṃ
pahāsiṃ rāgadosañ ca tadekaṭṭhe ca āsave.

100 bhikkhunī upasampajja pubbajātim anussariṃ
visodhitaṃ dibbacakkhuṃ vimalaṃ sādhubhāvitaṃ.

101 saṅkhāre parato disvā hetujāte palokite
pahāsiṃ āsave sabbe sītibhūtamhi nibbutā ti.

Sakula

I[11] was living at home when I heard the Buddha's teaching 97
from a monk,
and I saw the dhamma perfectly, knew freedom, the
eternal state.

Who I was then left behind son and daughter, wealth and 98
grain,
after cutting off my hair, I went forth to homelessness.

I trained myself, I developed the straight path, 99
I gave up excitement and anger
together with all that fouls the heart.

I ordained as a nun, I remembered former lives, 100
the eye that sees the invisible was clear, spotless,
developed.

I saw my experiences as if they were not my own, 101
born from a cause, destined to disappear.
I got rid of all that fouls the heart,
I am cool, free.

soṇā

102 dasa putte vijāyitvā asmiṃ rūpasamussaye
tatohaṃ dubbalā jiṇṇā bhikkhuniṃ upasaṅkamiṃ.

103 sā me dhammam adesesi khandhāyatanadhātuyo
tassā dhammaṃ suṇitvāna kese chetvāna pabbajiṃ.

104 tassā me sikkhamānāya dibbacakkhuṃ visodhitaṃ
pubbenivāsaṃ jānāmi yattha me vusitaṃ pure.

105 animittañ ca bhāvemi ekaggā susamāhitā
anantarā vimokkhāsiṃ anupādāya nibbutā.

106 pañcakkhandhā pariññātā tiṭṭhanti chinnamūlakā
dhitavatthu jare jamme natthi dāni punabbhavo ti.

Sona

It[12] was after I gave birth to ten sons with this body, 102
when I was weak and old that I approached a nun.

She taught me the dhamma 103
about what makes a person,
about the senses and their objects,
and about the basic elements that make up everything,[13]
and when I heard what she taught,
I cut off my hair and went forth.

By training under her, 104
my eye that sees the invisible became clear,
I knew my previous lives, where I had lived before.

I cultivated a state of mind 105
that depends on nothing else and cannot be measured,
I became focused, collected.
I am free, and I will always be completely free.

radox?! I know the five impersonal things 106
that make up a person,[14]
they may still stand, but their roots are cut.
The calamity now is for miserable old age itself:
I will not be reborn again.

↳ doesn't want to not live but her soul has reached enlightenment

bhaddā kuṇḍalakesā

107 lūnakesī paṅkadharī ekasāṭī pure cariṃ
avajje vajjamatinī vajje cā vajjadassinī.

108 divāvihārā nikkhamma gijjhakūṭamhi pabbate
addasaṃ virajaṃ buddhaṃ bhikkhusaṅghapurakkhataṃ.

109 nihacca jāṇuṃ vanditvā sammukhā pañjaliṃ akaṃ
ehi bhaddeti maṃ avaca sā me āsūpasampadā.

110 ciṇṇā aṅgā ca magadhā vajjī kāsī ca kosalā
anaṇā paṇṇāsavassāni raṭṭhapiṇḍaṃ abhuñjahaṃ.

111 puññaṃ ca pasavī bahuṃ sappañño vatāyaṃ upāsako
yo bhaddāya cīvaraṃ adāsi vippamuttāya sabbaganthehī
ti.

Bhadda Kundalakesa

Once[15] I wandered with hair cut off, 107
covered with dirt, wearing only one cloth,[16]
I thought there was a fault where there was none,
and I saw no fault where there were.

I went out from the day-shelter up Gijjhakuta mountain 108
where I saw the spotless Buddha honored by his monks.

I bent my knees and worshiped, 109
facing him I joined my hands in honor.
He said to me, "Come, Bhadda."
That was my ordination.

Chinna, Anga, Magadha, Vajji, Kasi, and Kosala— 110
for fifty years I enjoyed the alms of these places,
never incurring a debt.

The name I was called means good fortune, 111
it now becomes me.

That wise lay Buddhist made a lot of merit[17]
when he gave a robe to me,
this Bhadda, who is quite free from all ties.

paṭācārā

112 naṅgalehi kasaṃ khettaṃ bījāni pavapaṃ chamā
puttadārāni posentā dhanaṃ vindanti mānavā.[4]

113 kim ahaṃ sīlasampannā satthusāsanakārikā
nibbānaṃ nādhigacchāmi akusītā anuddhatā.

114 pāde pakkhālayitvāna udakesu karomahaṃ
pādodakañ ca disvāna thalato ninnam āgataṃ.

115 tato cittaṃ samādhesiṃ assaṃ bhadraṃ vajāniyaṃ
tato dīpaṃ gahetvāna vihāraṃ pāvisiṃ ahaṃ.

116 seyyaṃ olokayitvāna mañcakamhi upāvisiṃ
tato sūciṃ gahetvāna vaṭṭiṃ okassayāmahaṃ
padīpasseva nibbānaṃ vimokkho ahu cetaso ti.

Patachara

Furrowing[18] fields with plows, sowing seeds in the ground, 112
taking care of wives and children, young men find wealth.

So why have I not experienced freedom, 113
when I am virtuous and I do what the Teacher taught,
when I am not lazy and I am calm?

While washing my feet I made the water useful in another way, 114
by concentrating on it move from the higher ground down.

Then I held back my mind, 115
as one would do with a thoroughbred horse,
and I took a lamp and went into the hut.

First I looked at the bed, then I sat on the couch, 116
I used a needle to pull out the lamp's wick.
Just as the lamp went out, my mind was free.

tiṃsamattā

117 musalāni gahetvāna dhaññaṃ koṭṭenti mānavā
puttadārāni posentā dhanaṃ vindanti mānavā.[5]

118 karotha buddhasāsanaṃ yaṃ katvā nānutappati
khippaṃ pādāni dhovitvā ekamante nisīdatha
cetosamatham anuyuttā karotha buddhasāsanaṃ.

119 tassā tā vacanaṃ sutvā paṭācārāya sāsanaṃ
pāde pakkhālayitvāna ekamantaṃ upāvisuṃ
cetosamatham anuyuttā akaṃsu buddhasāsanaṃ.

120 rattiyā purime yāme pubbajātim anussaruṃ
rattiyā majjhime yāme dibbacakkhuṃ visodhayuṃ
rattiyā pacchime yāme tamokkhandhaṃ padālayuṃ.

A group of as many as thirty nuns

Spoken to them by Patachara

Young[19] men find wealth 117
taking sticks and threshing grain,
taking care of wives and children.

Do what the Buddha taught, 118
there's nothing to be sorry for after doing it.
Quick, wash the feet, sit down off to one side.
Intent on calming the mind, do what the Buddha taught.

Spoken by Patachara's students about themselves

They heard her words, what Patachara taught, 119
they washed their feet, sat down off to one side,
intent on calming the mind, they did what the Buddha taught.

In the first watch of the night, they remembered their previous lives, 120
in the middle watch, they cleansed the eye that sees the invisible,
in the last watch of the night,
they split open the mass of mental darkness.

121 uṭṭhāya pāde vandiṃsu katā te anusāsanī
indaṃ va devā tidasā saṅgāme aparājitaṃ
purakkhatvā vihariyāma[6] tevijjamha anāsavā[7] ti.

candā

122 duggatāhaṃ pure āsiṃ vidhavā ca aputtikā
vinā mittehi ñātīhi bhattacoḷassa nādhigaṃ.

123 pattaṃ daṇḍañ ca gaṇhitvā bhikkhamānā kulākulaṃ
sītuṇhena ca ḍayhantī satta vassāni cārihaṃ.

124 bhikkhuniṃ puna disvāna annapānassa lābhiniṃ
upasaṅkammāvocaṃ pabbajjaṃ anagāriyaṃ.

125 sā ca maṃ anukampāya pabbājesi paṭācārā
tato maṃ ovaditvāna paramatthe niyojayi.

126 tassāhaṃ vacanaṃ sutvā akāsiṃ anusāsaniṃ
amoghoyyāya ovādo tevijjamhi anāsavā ti.

Standing up, they worshiped Patachara's feet, 121
and they said, "Your advice has been done,
we will live honoring you, like the thirty deities
honoring Indra, who is unconquered by others in battle.
We know the three things that most don't know,[20]
nothing fouls our hearts."

Chanda

In[21] the past, I was poor, a widow, without children, 122
without friends or relatives, I did not get food or clothing.

Taking a bowl and stick, I went begging from family to family, 123
I wandered for seven years, tormented by cold and heat.

Then I saw a nun as she was receiving food and drink. 124
Approaching her, I said, "Make me go forth to homelessness."

And she was sympathetic to me and Patachara made me go forth, 125
she gave me advice and pointed me toward the highest goal.

I listened to her words and I put into action her advice. 126
That excellent woman's advice was not empty,
I know the three things that most don't know,[22]
nothing fouls my heart.

chakkanipāto

pañcasatamattā

127 yassa maggaṃ na jānāsi āgatassa gatassa vā
taṃ kuto āgataṃ sattaṃ mama putto ti rodasi.

128 maggaṃ ca khossa jānāsi āgatassa gatassa vā
na naṃ samanusocesi evaṃ dhammā hi pāṇino.

129 ayācito tatāgacchi ananuññāto ito gato
kuto pi nūna āgantvā vasitvā katipāhakaṃ.

130 ito pi aññena gato tato apaññena gacchati
peto manussarūpena saṃsaranto gamissati
yathāgato tathā gato kā tattha paridevanā.

POEMS WITH SIX VERSES

A group of as many as five hundred nuns
Spoken to them by Patachara

You[1] keep crying out, "My son!" 127
to that being who was coming or going somewhere else
and who came from somewhere else,
none of which you know.

But you do not really cry for him 128
over what you do know will face him wherever he is:
that is just human nature.

He came from there uninvited, he went from here without permission, 129
he came from somewhere or other, he stayed a bit.

From here he went one way, from there he will go another, 130
a hungry ghost will be reborn as a human.
He went the way he came, what is there to grieve about?

131 abbahī vata me sallaṃ duddasaṃ hadayassitaṃ
yā me sokaparetāya puttasokaṃ vyapānudi.

132 sājja abbūḷhasallāhaṃ nicchātā parinibbutā
buddhaṃ dhammaṃ ca saṅghaṃ ca upemi saraṇaṃ
munin ti.

Spoken by each of them one by one, repeating
what Patachara herself said

She pulled out the arrow that was hard for me to see, 131
the one that I nourished in my heart,
she expelled the grief for a son,
the grief that had overwhelmed me.

Today the arrow is pulled out, 132
I am without hunger, completely free.
I go to the Buddha, his dhamma, and his sangha[2] for
refuge,
I go to the Sage for refuge.

vāseṭṭhī

133 puttasokenahaṃ aṭṭā khittacittā visaññinī
naggā pakiṇṇakesī ca tena tena vicārihaṃ.

134 vasiṃ saṅkārakūṭesu susāne rathiyāsu ca
acariṃ tīṇi vassāni khuppipāsā samappitā.

135 athaddasāsiṃ sugataṃ nagaraṃ mithilaṃ pati
adantānaṃ dametāraṃ sambuddham akuto bhayaṃ.

136 sacittaṃ paṭiladdhāna vanditvāna upāvisiṃ
so me dhammam adesesi anukampāya gotamo.

137 tassa dhammaṃ suṇitvāna pabbajiṃ anagāriyaṃ
yuñjantī satthu vacane sacchākāsiṃ padaṃ sivaṃ.

138 sabbe sokā samucchinnā pahīnā etadantikā
pariññātā hi me vatthū yato sokānasambhavo ti.

Vasetthi

I[3] was wounded by grief for my son, 133
mind unhinged, mad,
without clothes, hair unkempt,
I walked from place to place.

Resting on heaps of garbage in the streets, 134
in cemeteries, on highways
I wandered for three years,
always hungry and thirsty.

Then I saw the Sugata[4] going toward Mithila, 135
tamer of the untamed, fully awake, afraid of no one and nothing.

Back in my right mind, I worshiped him and came close. 136
Gotama[5] taught me the dhamma out of kindness toward me.

I listened to what he taught, I went forth to homelessness, 137
forming myself with what the Teacher said.
I knew at first hand the blissful state.

All sorrows are cut off, left behind, 138
this is their end,
now I understand things,
how could sorrow start again?

khemā

139 daharā tvaṃ rūpavatī aham pi daharo yuvā
pañcaṅgikena turiyena ehi kheme ramāmase.

140 iminā pūtikāyena āturena pabhaṅgunā
aṭṭiyāmi harāyāmi kāmataṇhā samūhatā.[1]

141 sattisūlūpamā kāmā khandhāsaṃ adhikuṭṭanā
yaṃ tvaṃ kāmaratiṃ brūsi aratī dāni sā mama.[2]

142 sabbattha vihatā nandī tamokkhandho padālito
evaṃ jānāhi pāpima nihato tvam asi antaka.[3]

143 nakkhattāni namassantā aggiṃ paricaraṃ vane
yathābhuccaṃ ajānantā bālā suddhiṃ amaññatha.

144 ahañ ca kho namassantī sambuddhaṃ purisuttamaṃ
parimuttā sabbadukkhehi satthusāsanakārikā ti.

Khema

Spoken by Mara to her

You[6] are young and beautiful and so am I, 139
come, Khema, let's enjoy each other, make music together.

Khema replied

This foul body, sick, so easily broken, vexes and shames me, 140
my craving for sex has been rooted out.

The pleasures of sex are like swords and stakes, 141
the body, senses, and the mind
just the chopping block on which they cut.
What you call the delights of sexual pleasure
are no delights for me now.

What you take as pleasures are not for me, 142
the mass of mental darkness is split open.
Know this, evil one, you are defeated, you are finished.

You honor the stars, 143
look to them for guidance,
you tend the fire[7] in the forest.
Fools, you thought all that could be relied on,
all the while not knowing what really is.

But I honor the Buddha, best of all men. 144
By doing what the Buddha taught
I am freed from all sufferings.

sujātā

145 alaṅkatā suvasanā mālinī candanokkhitā
sabbābharaṇasañchannā dāsīgaṇapurakkhatā.

146 annaṃ pānañ ca ādāya khajjaṃ bhojjaṃ anappakaṃ
gehato nikkhamitvāna uyyānam abhihārayiṃ.

147 tattha ramitvā kīḷitvā āgacchantī sakaṃ gharaṃ
vihāraṃ daṭṭhuṃ pāvisiṃ sākete añjanaṃ vanaṃ.

148 disvāna lokapajjotaṃ vanditvāna upāvisiṃ
so me dhammam adesesi anukampāya cakkhumā.

149 sutvā ca kho mahesissa saccaṃ sampaṭivijjhahaṃ [4]
tattheva virajaṃ dhammaṃ phusayiṃ amataṃ padaṃ.

150 tato viññātasaddhammā pabbajiṃ anagāriyaṃ
tisso vijjā anuppattā amoghaṃ buddhasāsanan ti.

Sujata

I[8] was well dressed and dressed up, 145
covered with garlands and sandalwood paste,
wearing everything I could put on,
my servants waiting on me.

Taking food and drink, 146
all kinds of food and lots of it
I went from the house
and up to the garden.

After I enjoyed myself there, playing, 147
while on my way back home,
I went into the Anjana woods near Saketa
to see the monastery.

What I saw was the light of the world, 148
I worshiped first, then I came near.
The one who has an eye to see what others don't
taught me the dhamma out of kindness toward me.

I mastered what I heard, the dhamma of the great sage, 149
right there, I touched dhamma, spotless as it is,
I reached the place without death.

I knew the dhamma, I went forth to homelessness, 150
I know the three things that most don't know:[9]
what the Buddha taught is not useless.

anopamā

151 ucce kule ahaṃ jātā bahuvitte mahaddhane
vaṇṇarūpena sampannā dhītā meghassa[5] atrajā.

152 patthitā rājaputtehi seṭṭhiputtehibhijjhitā
pitu me pesayī dūtaṃ detha mayhaṃ anopamaṃ.

153 yattakaṃ tulitā esā tuyhaṃ dhītā anopamā
tato aṭṭhaguṇaṃ dassaṃ hiraññaṃ ratanāni ca.

154 sāhaṃ disvāna sambuddhaṃ lokajeṭṭhaṃ anuttaraṃ
tassa pādāni vanditvā ekamantaṃ upāvisiṃ.

155 so me dhammam adesesi anukampāya gotamo
nisinnā āsane tasmiṃ phusayiṃ tatiyaṃ phalaṃ.

156 tato kesāni chetvāna pabbajiṃ anagāriyaṃ
ajja me sattamī ratti yato taṇhā visositā ti.

Anopama

I[10] was born in a good family with great wealth and many possessions; 151
good looking, I was Megha's very own daughter.

I lived up to my name which means "without compare."

I was sought after by princes, coveted by sons of millionaires, 152
until one sent my father a message: "Give me Anopama.

"I will give eight times what your daughter Anopama 153
weighs in gold and silver as bride price."

I saw the Buddha, supreme in the world, unsurpassed, 154
I worshiped his feet, then I came near on one side.

Gotama taught me the dhamma out of kindness toward me, 155
and sitting there, I became one who would not return again.

I cut my hair and went forth to homelessness, 156
today is the seventh night since craving was destroyed for me.

mahāpajāpatigotamī

157 buddhavīra namo tyatthu sabbasattānam uttama
yo maṃ dukkhā pamocesi aññaṃ ca bahukaṃ janaṃ.

158 sabbadukkhaṃ pariññātaṃ hetutaṇhā visositā
āriyaṭṭhaṅgiko[6] maggo nirodho phusito mayā.

159 mātā putto pitā bhātā ayyakā ca pure ahuṃ
yathābhuccam ajānantī saṃsariṃhaṃ anibbisaṃ.

160 diṭṭho hi me so bhagavā antimoyaṃ samussayo
vikkhīṇo jātisaṃsāro natthi dāni punabbhavo.

161 āraddhaviriye pahitatte niccaṃ daḷhaparakkame
samagge sāvake passe esā buddhāna vandanā.

Mahapajapati Gotami

Praise[11] to you, hero among Buddhas,[12] best of all beings, 157
you freed me from suffering, just as you did so many other people.

All suffering is known, 158
the craving that is suffering's cause has been destroyed,
the eightfold path of the noble ones has been traveled
and cessation reached:

the four noble truths
each one done
all done by me.

I had already been a mother, a son, 159
a father, a brother, and a grandmother,
but not knowing things as they really are,
I was reborn and reborn,
never having enough.

As soon as I saw the Bhagavan,[13] I knew that this is my last body, 160
that the realm of births is finished, that now there is no rebirth for me.

When I look at the disciples assembled together, 161
energetic, resolute, always making an effort,
I see that this is how Buddhas are rightly worshiped.

162 bahūnaṃ vata atthāya māyā janayi gotamaṃ
vyādhimaraṇatunnānaṃ dukkhakkhandhaṃ vyapānudī ti.

guttā

163 gutte yadatthaṃ pabbajjā hitvā puttaṃ vasuṃ piyaṃ
tam eva anubrūhehi mā cittassa vasaṃ gami.

164 cittena vañcitā sattā mārassa visaye ratā
anekajātisaṃsāraṃ sandhāvanti aviddasū.

165 kāmacchandañ ca vyāpādaṃ sakkāyadiṭṭhim eva ca
sīlabbataparāmāsaṃ vicikicchañ ca pañcamaṃ.

166 saññojanāni etāni pajahitvāna bhikkhunī
oraṃbhāgamanīyāni nayidaṃ punarehisi.

167 rāgaṃ mānaṃ avijjañ ca uddhaccaṃ ca vivajjiya
saññojanāni chetvāna dukkhassantaṃ karissasi.

Mahamaya gave birth to Gotama for the sake of many, 162
to drive away the mass of suffering
of all those struck down by sickness and death.

Gutta

Spoken by the Buddha to her and then repeated by her after enlightenment

Gutta,[14] practice what you went forth for, 163
after you gave up your son and your wealth, all that is dear.
Don't let your mind control you.

Those who are deceived by their minds 164
delight in Mara's realm,
endlessly reborn, always remaining ignorant.

There are five fetters that bind one to misery: 165
the urge for sex, intense ill will, thinking that one has a soul,
being attached to useless practices, and doubt is the fifth.

O nun, if you throw off these fetters, 166
which always lead to lower realms of rebirth,
you will not come to this state again.

Turn away from passion and pride, ignorance and racing thoughts, 167
cut the fetters and you will put an end to suffering.

168 khepetvā jātisaṃsāraṃ pariññāya punabbhavaṃ
diṭṭheva dhamme nicchātā upasantā carissatī ti.

vijayā

169 catukkhattuṃ pañcakkhattuṃ vihārā upanikkhamiṃ
aladdhā cetaso santiṃ citte avasavattinī.[7]

170 bhikkhuniṃ upasaṅkamma sakkaccaṃ paripucchahaṃ
sā me dhammam adesesi dhātuāyatanāni ca.

171 cattāri ariyasaccāni indriyāni balāni ca
bojjhaṅgaṭṭhaṅgikaṃ maggaṃ uttamatthassa pattiyā.

172 tassāhaṃ vacanaṃ sutvā karontī anusāsaniṃ
rattiyā purime yāme pubbajātim anussariṃ.

173 rattiyā majjhime yāme dibbacakkhuṃ visodhayiṃ
rattiyā pacchime yāme tamokkhandhaṃ padālayiṃ.

Free yourself from birth after birth, 168
really comprehend rebirth,
and you will move among things,
calm and satisfied with them just as they are.

Vijaya

Four[15] times, five times, I went out from the monastery, 169
with no peace in my heart, no control over my mind.

I approached a nun, honored her, questioned her. 170
She taught me the dhamma about physicality and the
senses,

about the four noble truths, 171
about how we know what we know,[16]
and powers that can be cultivated,
about what brings us to awakening,
the eightfold path to the highest goal.

I listened to what she said and did what she taught, 172
in the first watch of the night, I remembered my previous
births,

in the middle watch, I became able to see what was not 173
visible,
and in the last watch, I split open the mass of mental
darkness.

174 pītisukhena ca kāyaṃ pharitvā vihariṃ tadā
sattamiyā pāde pasāresiṃ tamokkhandhaṃ padāliyā ti.

And so I lived, filling my body with joy and happiness, 174
seven days after splitting open the mass of mental
darkness,
I stretched out my feet.

sattakanipāto

uttarā

175 musalāni gahetvāna dhaññaṃ koṭṭenti mānavā
puttadārāni posentā dhanaṃ vindanti mānavā.[1]

176 ghaṭetha buddhasāsane yaṃ katvā nānutappati
khippaṃ pādāni dhovitvā ekamantaṃ nisīdatha.

177 cittaṃ upaṭṭhapetvāna ekaggaṃ susamāhitaṃ
paccavekkhatha saṅkhāre parato no ca attato.

178 tassāhaṃ vacanaṃ sutvā paṭācārānusāsaniṃ
pāde pakkhālayitvāna ekamante upāvisiṃ.

179 rattiyā purime yāme pubbajātimanussariṃ
rattiyā majjhime yāme dibbacakkhuṃ visodhayiṃ.

180 rattiyā pacchime yāme tamokkhandhaṃ padālayiṃ
tevijjā atha vuṭṭhāsiṃ katā te anusāsanī.

POEMS WITH SEVEN VERSES

Uttara

"Young[1] men find wealth 175
taking sticks and threshing grain,
taking care of wives and children.

"Do what the Buddha taught, 176
there's nothing to be sorry for after doing it.
Quick, wash the feet, sit down off to one side.

"Prepare the mind, make it intent, concentrated; 177
look at what your mind constructs
as coming from elsewhere, not from yourself."

I listened to the advice that Patachara gave, 178
I then washed my feet and came near on one side.

In the first watch of the night, I remembered my previous births, 179
in the middle watch, I became able to see what was not visible.

In the last watch, I split open the mass of mental darkness, 180
and when I stood up
I knew the three things that most don't know.[2]
What you advised, I had done.

181 sakkaṃ va devā tidasā saṅgāme aparājitaṃ
purakkhatvā viharāmi[2] tevijjamhi anāsavā[3] ti.

cālā

182 satiṃ upaṭṭhapetvāna bhikkhunī bhāvitindriyā
paṭivijjhi padaṃ santaṃ saṅkhārūpasamaṃ sukhaṃ.

183 kan nu uddissa muṇḍāsi samaṇī viya dissasi
na ca rocesi pāsaṇḍe kim idaṃ carasi momuhā.

184 ito bahiddhā pāsaṇḍā diṭṭhiyo upanissitā
na te dhammaṃ vijānanti na te dhammassa kovidā.

So I live, 181
knowing the three things most don't know,
nothing fouling the heart,
honoring you in the same way
that the thirty deities honor Sakka,[3]
who was unconquered by others in battle.

Chala

After[4] I had cultivated mindfulness, 182
and was already a nun who knew well how to know,[5]
I entered the place of peace,
where all mental constructions are stilled,
which is happiness itself.

Then Mara spoke to me:

Who is to blame for your shaved head? 183
You look like an ascetic,
but it looks like you don't like being with other ascetics.
Why are you doing this, silly woman?

I answered Mara:

Those other ascetics are strangers to me, they rely on false views, 184
they do not know the dhamma, they don't know about reality.

185 atthi sakyakule jāto buddho appaṭipuggalo
so me dhammam adesesi diṭṭhīnaṃ samatikkamaṃ.

186 dukkhaṃ dukkhasamuppādaṃ dukkhassa ca atikkamaṃ
ariyaṃ caṭṭhaṅgikaṃ maggaṃ dukkhūpasamagāminaṃ.

187 tassāhaṃ vacanaṃ sutvā vihariṃ sāsane ratā
tisso vijjā anuppattā kataṃ buddhassa sāsanaṃ.[4]

188 sabbattha vihatā nandī tamokkhandho padālito
evaṃ jānāhi pāpima nihato tvam asi antakā[5] ti.

The Buddha who was born among the Sakyas, 185
he is without peer,
he taught me the dhamma
that is far beyond all false views.

He taught me about suffering, 186
how suffering comes to be,
and how one goes beyond it;
he taught the noble eightfold path
that goes to the stilling of suffering.[6]

After I heard what he said, I lived 187
delighting in his teaching.
I have seen with my own eyes
the three things that most don't know,[7]
what the Buddha taught is done.

What you take as pleasures are not for me, 188
the mass of mental darkness is split open.
Know this, evil one, you are defeated, you are finished.

upacālā

189 satimatī cakkhumatī bhikkhunī bhāvitindriyā
paṭivijjhiṃ padaṃ santaṃ akāpurisasevitaṃ.

190 kinnu jātiṃ na rocesi jāto kāmāni bhuñjati
bhuñjāhi kāmaratiyo māhu pacchānutāpinī.

191 jātassa maraṇaṃ hoti hatthapādāna chedanaṃ
vadhabandhapariklesaṃ jāto dukkhaṃ nigacchati.

192 atthi sakyakule jāto sambuddho aparājito
so me dhammam adesesi jātiyā samatikkamam.

Upachala

Spoken at Upachala's enlightenment

Mindful,[8] having the eye of wisdom, 189
already a nun who knew how to know well.[9]
I entered the state of peace
that is enjoyed by noble people.

Spoken by Mara to her

Why not delight in life? 190
Everyone alive enjoys physical pleasures,
enjoy the pleasures of sex now,
you won't regret it later.

Upachala replied

Death comes to everyone born, 191
and until that happens
hands and feet are cut off,
there is bondage and execution and other misery,
birth brings suffering.

The Buddha who was born among the Sakyas, 192
unconquered,
he taught me the dhamma
that goes far beyond birth.

193 dukkhaṃ dukkhasamuppādaṃ dukkhassa ca atikkamaṃ
ariyañ caṭṭhaṅgikaṃ maggaṃ dukkhūpasamagāminaṃ.

194 tassāhaṃ vacanaṃ sutvā vihariṃ sāsane ratā
tisso vijjā anuppattā kataṃ buddhassa sāsanaṃ.[6]

195 sabbattha vihatā nandī tamokkhandho padālito
evaṃ jānāhi pāpima nihato tvam asi antakā[7] ti.

He taught me about suffering, 193
how suffering comes to be,
and how one goes beyond it;
he taught the noble eightfold path
that goes to the stilling of suffering.[10]

After I heard what he said, I lived 194
delighting in his teaching.
I have seen with my own eyes
the three things that most don't know,[11]
what the Buddha taught is done.

What you take as pleasures are not for me, 195
the mass of mental darkness is split open.
Know this, evil one, you are defeated, you are finished.

aṭṭhakanipāto

sīsūpacālā

196 bhikkhunī sīlasampannā indriyesu susaṃvutā
adhigacche padaṃ santaṃ asecanakamojavaṃ.

197 tāvatiṃsā ca yāmā ca tusitā cāpi devatā
nimmānaratino devā ye devā vasavattino
tattha cittaṃ paṇīdhehi yattha te vusitaṃ pure.[1]

198 tāvatiṃsā ca yāmā ca tusitā cāpi devatā
nimmānaratino devā ye devā vasavattino.

199 kālaṃ kālaṃ bhavābhavaṃ sakkā yasmiṃ purakkhatā
avītivattā sakkāyaṃ jātimaraṇasārino.

A POEM WITH EIGHT VERSES

Sisupachala

Spoken at Sisupachala's enlightenment

The[1] nun filled with virtues, 196
with the ways we know the world[2] well-controlled,
attains the state of peace, sublime and sweet.

Spoken by Mara to her

There are gods in the Tavatimsa heaven, 197
Yama gods, and also ones in the Tusita realm,
gods who create their own pleasures
and gods who enjoy what others create,[3]
turn your mind to the pleasures of those places
that you once enjoyed.

Sisupachala replied

There are still gods in the Tavatimsa heaven, 198
Yama gods, and also ones in the Tusita realm,
gods who create their own pleasures
and gods who enjoy what others create,

but all of them, time and again, life after life, 199
in whatever body they come to be,
never get beyond embodiment,
they just run after more birth and death.

200 sabbo ādīpito loko sabbo loko padīpito
sabbo pajjalito loko sabbo loko pakampito.

201 akampiyaṃ atuliyaṃ aputhujjanasevitaṃ
buddho dhammam adesesi tattha me nirato mano.

202 tassāhaṃ vacanaṃ sutvā vihariṃ sāsane ratā
tisso vijjā anuppattā kataṃ buddhassa sāsanaṃ.[2]

203 sabbattha vihatā nandī tamokkhandho padālito
evaṃ jānāhi pāpima nihato tvam asi antakā[3] ti.

The whole world is in flames, the whole world is burning, 200
the whole world is blazing, the whole world is shaking.

The Buddha taught the dhamma that cannot be shaken. 201
It has no equal
and is not known by ordinary people,
but I have fixed the mind on it.

After I heard what he said, I lived 202
delighting in his teaching.
I have seen with my own eyes
the three things that most don't know,[4]
what the Buddha taught is done.

What you take as pleasures are not for me, 203
the mass of mental darkness is split open.
Know this, evil one, you are defeated, you are finished.

navakanipāto

vaḍḍhamātu

204 mā su te vaḍḍha lokamhi vanatho ahu kudācanaṃ
mā puttaka punappunaṃ ahu dukkhassa bhāgimā.

205 sukhaṃ hi vaḍḍha munayo anejā chinnasaṃsayā
sītibhūtā damappattā viharanti anāsavā.

206 tehānuciṇṇaṃ isībhi maggaṃ dassanapattiyā
dukkhassantakiriyāya tvaṃ vaḍḍha anubrūhaya.

207 visāradā va bhaṇasi etam atthaṃ janetti me
maññāmi nūna māmike vanatho te na vijjati.

208 ye keci vaḍḍha saṅkhārā hīnā ukkaṭṭhamajjhimā
aṇū pi aṇumatto pi vanatho me na vijjati.

A POEM WITH NINE VERSES

Vaddha's mother
Spoken to her son

Vaddha,[1] may you never have any lust in this world 204
and may you not partake of suffering over and over.

Sages live happily, 205
free from desire,
doubts dispelled, cooled, tamed,
nothing oozing out from within, Vaddha.

Vaddha, may you practice the path those rishis did 206
the path that gives insight and puts an end to suffering.

Vaddha, knowing his mother was now enlightened, said
Mother, it's clear to me 207
that you know what you are talking about,
you are the one who gave me birth,
but I am the one who is sure
that desire does not exist in you.

His mother replied
Whatever there may be 208
whose existence is because of something else,
no matter how low, high, or in-between,
no matter how small or minute,
I have no desire for it.

209 sabbe me āsavā khīṇā appamattassa jhāyato
tisso vijjā anuppattā kataṃ buddhassa sāsanaṃ.

210 uḷāraṃ vata me mātā patodaṃ samavassari
paramatthasaṃhitā gāthā yathā pi anukampikā.

211 tassāhaṃ vacanaṃ sutvā anusiṭṭhiṃ janettiyā
dhammasaṃvegam āpādiṃ yogakkhemassa pattiyā.

212 sohaṃ padhānapahitatto rattindivam atandito
mātarā codito santo aphusiṃ santim uttaman ti.

Every depravity that can ooze out from within is already gone, 209
I go on making an effort and meditating,[2]
I have seen with my own eyes
the three things that most don't know,[3]
what the Buddha taught is done.

Vaddha then said

It seemed like she wielded a driving goad, 210
when my mother, out of kindness
urged me forward
with verses about the highest goal.

I heard her words, 211
instruction by the one who gave me birth,
and I felt a profound urgency to reach the state of freedom.

Making an effort, intent, not relaxing day or night, 212
urged on by my mother, I reached the highest peace.

ekādasanipāto

kisāgotamī

213 kalyāṇamittatā muninā lokaṃ ādissa vaṇṇitā
kalyāṇamitte bhajamāno api bālo paṇḍito assa.

214 bhajitabbā sappurisā paññā tathā vaḍḍhati bhajantānaṃ
bhajamāno sappurise sabbehi pi dukkhehi pamucceyya.

215 dukkhaṃ ca vijāneyya dukkhassa ca samudayaṃ nirodhaṃ
aṭṭhaṅgikañ ca maggaṃ cattāri pi ariyasaccāni.

216 dukkho itthibhāvo akkhāto purisadammasārathinā
sapattikam pi hi dukkhaṃ appekaccā sakiṃ vijātāyo.

A POEM WITH ELEVEN VERSES

Kisagotami

Kisagotami speaks remembering all that she attained because of the good friendship of the Buddha

The[1] Sage commended having good friends 213
for anyone anywhere in the universe.
By keeping company with good friends
even a fool becomes wise.

Keep company with good people, 214
wisdom increases for those who do.
By keeping company with good people
one is freed from every suffering.

One should know suffering, 215
the origin of suffering and its cessation,
the eightfold path.[2]

A female deity speaks about the state of being a woman

Being a woman is suffering, 216
that has been shown by the Buddha,
the tamer of those to be tamed.

Sharing a husband with another wife is suffering for some,
while for others, having a baby just once is more than
enough suffering.

217 galake api kantanti sukhumāliniyo visāni khādanti
janamārakam ajjhagatā ubho pi vyasanāni anubhonti.

218 upavijaññā gacchantī addasāhaṃ patiṃ mataṃ
panthamhi vijāyitvāna appattā va sakaṃ gharaṃ.

219 dve puttā kālakatā patī ca panthe mato kapaṇikāya
mātā pitā ca bhātā ḍayhanti ca ekacitakāyaṃ.

220 khīṇakulīne kapaṇe anubhūtaṃ te dukkhaṃ aparimāṇaṃ
assū ca te pavattaṃ bahūni ca jātisahassāni.

221 vasitā susānamajjhe atho pi khāditāni puttamaṃsāni
hatakulikā sabbagarahitā matapatikā amataṃ adhigacchi.[1]

Some women cut their throats, 217
others take poison,
some die in pregnancy
and then both mother and child experience miseries.

Kisagotami herself speaks about the dangers of being a woman, by telling the story of Patachara

About to deliver 218
while still on the way,
I found my husband dead
right there on the road;
I gave birth
before I reached home.

The two sons of this wretched woman 219
too soon dead, her husband dead too
right there on the road,
even while her mother, father, and brother
were burned on one funeral pyre.

Kisagotami continues about herself

Wretched woman, your family is dead too, 220
suffering without end has been yours,
your tears have flowed
for thousands of births.

After living in the middle of a cemetery 221
the bodies of her sons now only something eaten,
family destroyed, despised by all, husband dead,
she reached what is without death.

222 bhāvito me maggo ariyo aṭṭhaṅgiko amatagāmī
nibbānaṃ sacchikataṃ dhammādāsaṃ apekkhihaṃ.[2]

223 aham amhi kantasallā ohitabhārā kataṃ hi karaṇīyaṃ
kisāgotamī therī vimuttacittā imaṃ abhaṇī ti.

I followed the noble eightfold path 222
that goes to that which is without death,
nibbana is known at first hand.
I have seen myself in the mirror of the dhamma.

Now I am someone 223
with depravities' darts cut out,
with burden laid down,
who has done what needs to be done.

The nun Kisagotami
her mind freed
said this.

dvādasakanipāto

uppalavaṇṇā

224 ubho mātā ca dhītā ca mayaṃ āsuṃ sapattiyo
tassā me ahu saṃvego abbhuto lomahaṃsano.

225 dhiratthu kāmā asucī duggandhā bahukaṇṭakā
yattha mātā ca dhītā ca sabhariyā mayaṃ ahuṃ.

226 kāmesvādīnavaṃ disvā nekkhammaṃ daṭṭhu khemato
sā pabbajji rājagahe agārasmānagāriyaṃ.

227 pubbenivāsaṃ jānāmi dibbacakkhuṃ visodhitaṃ
cetopariccañāṇañca sotadhātu visodhitā.[1]

A POEM WITH TWELVE VERSES

Uppalavanna

Remembering another's story when she saw the dangers in sexual urges

We[1] were mother and daughter, 224
but we shared one husband,
I was afraid of what had to come from that,
it was perverse and made my hair stand on end.

Sexual urges, let them be cursed, 225
they are dirty, foul, dangerous,
and they were all right there
where mother and daughter shared one husband.

Seeing the dangers in sexual urges 226
and looking at freedom from lust
from the standpoint of safety,
she went forth in Rajagaha,
from home to homelessness.

Spoken by her as she looked back over her attainments

I know my previous lives 227
and the eye that can see the invisible is clear,
I know the ways of my heart, now I hear clearly.

228 iddhī pi me sacchikatā patto me āsavakkhayo
chaḷabhiññā sacchikatā kataṃ buddhassa sāsanaṃ.[2]

229 iddhiyā abhinimmitvā caturassaṃ rathaṃ ahaṃ
buddhassa pāde vanditvā lokanāthassa tādino.

230 supupphitaggaṃ upagamma pādapaṃ ekā tuvaṃ tiṭṭhasi
sālamūle
na cāpi te dutiyo atthi koci na tvaṃ bāle bhāyasi
dhuttakānaṃ.

231 sataṃ sahassāni pi dhuttakānaṃ samāgatā edisakā
bhaveyyuṃ
lomaṃ na iñje na pi sampavedhe kiṃ me tuvaṃ māra
karissaseko.

Powers beyond normal I knew at first hand, 228
the depravities that ooze out from within have wasted away,
the six powers[2] attained, the teaching of the Buddha is done.

Spoken by her to the Buddha at the time of the twin miracle

With those powers, I produced from nothing 229
a chariot with four horses,
I worshiped the feet of the Buddha,
the protector of the world like no other.

Spoken to her by Mara when he saw her resting one day

You came to this tree in full bloom 230
and you now stand there
all alone at the foot of a *sala* tree,
no one else here.
Foolish child, aren't you afraid of rakes?

Uppalavanna replied

Even if a hundred thousand scamps were to come 231
I would not turn a hair, nor would I flinch one bit.
So, Mara, what will you do,
when it is just you all by yourself?

232 esā antaradhāyāmi kucchiṃ vā pavisāmi te
bhamukantare va tiṭṭhāmi tiṭṭhantiṃ maṃ na dakkhasi.

233 cittamhi vasībhūtāhaṃ iddhipādā subhāvitā
cha me abhiññā sacchikatā kataṃ buddhassa sāsanaṃ.

234 sattisūlūpamā kāmā khandhāsaṃ adhikuṭṭanā
yaṃ tvaṃ kāmaratiṃ brūsi aratī dāni sā mama.[3]

235 sabbattha vihatā nandī tamokkhandho padālito
evaṃ jānāhi pāpima nihato tvam asi antakā[4] ti.

Maybe I will just disappear 232
or maybe I will get inside your belly,
maybe I will stand between your eyebrows,
but wherever it may be,
you won't see
where I am standing.

I have my mind under control, 233
powers beyond normal are mine to use,
the six powers[3] have been attained by me,
the teaching of the Buddha is done.

The pleasures of sex are like swords and stakes, 234
the body, senses, and the mind
just the chopping block on which they cut.
What you call the delights of sexual pleasure
are no delights for me now.

What you take as pleasures are not for me, 235
the mass of mental darkness is split open.
Know this, evil one, you are defeated, you are finished.

soḷasanipāto

puṇṇā

236 udakam āhariṃ sīte sadā udakam otariṃ
ayyānaṃ daṇḍabhayabhītā vācādosabhayaṭṭitā.

237 kassa brāhmaṇa tvaṃ bhīto sadā udakam otari
vedhamānehi gattehi sītaṃ vedayase bhusaṃ.

238 jānantī vata maṃ bhoti puṇṇike paripucchasi
karontaṃ kusalaṃ kammaṃ rundhantaṃ katapāpakaṃ.

239 yo ca vuḍḍho daharo vā pāpakammaṃ pakubbati
dakābhisecanā so pi pāpakammā pamuccati.

A POEM WITH SIXTEEN VERSES

Punna

Punna speaks to a Brahman

I[1] carried water, 236
even when it was cold
I still went down into the water,
afraid of the sticks of my mistresses,
afraid of their words and their anger.

But what are you afraid of, Brahman 237
when you go into the water,
your body shivering
as you feel the biting cold?

The Brahman answers

Even though you know me, Punnika 238
you still ask why I am doing
this skillful act,
blocking the fruits of the evil already done.

Anyone who does an evil act, 239
whether old or young,
is freed from the fruits of that evil act
by washing off in water.

240 ko nu te idam akkhāsi ajānantassa ajānako
dakābhisecanā nāma pāpakammā pamuccati.

241 saggaṃ nūna gamissanti sabbe maṇḍūkakacchapā
nakkā[1] ca suṃsumārā ca ye caññe udake carā.

242 orabbhikā sūkarikā macchikā migabandhakā
corā ca vajjhaghātā ca ye caññe pāpakammino.

243 dakābhisecanā te pi pāpakammā pamuccare
sace imā nadiyo te pāpaṃ pubbe kataṃ vahuṃ.

244 puññānimāni vaheyyuṃ te tena tvaṃ paribāhiro
yassa brāhmaṇa tvaṃ bhīto sadā udakam otari.

245 tvam eva brahme mākāsi mā te sītaṃ chaviṃ hane
kummaggapaṭipannaṃ maṃ ariyamaggaṃ samānayi.

Punna

Who told you that, 240
like a know-nothing speaking to a know-nothing,
that one is freed from the fruits of an evil act
by washing off in water?

Is it that frogs and turtles 241
will all go to heaven,
and so will water monitors and crocodiles,
and anything that lives in water,

as will killers of sheep and killers of pigs, 242
fishermen and animal trappers,
thieves and executioners,
everyone who habitually does evil?

They are freed from the fruits of their evil acts 243
if these rivers can just carry away the evil already done?

But these rivers might carry away all the good done too, 244
you'll be besides yourself about that,
aren't you afraid of that, Brahman,
each time you go down into the water?

The Brahman

When you told me, 245
"Don't do it, don't let the cold strike your skin,"
you led me who was on the wrong path
to the path of those who are noble,

246 dakābhisecanā bhoti imaṃ sāṭaṃ dadāmi te
tuyheva sāṭako hotu nāham icchāmi sāṭakaṃ.

247 sace bhāyasi dukkhassa sace te dukkham appiyaṃ
mākāsi pāpakaṃ kammaṃ āvi vā yadi vā raho.[2]

248 sace ca pāpakaṃ kammaṃ karissasi karosi vā
na te dukkhā pamuttyatthi upeccā pi palāyato.

249 sace bhāyasi dukkhassa sace te dukkham appiyaṃ
upehi saraṇaṃ buddhaṃ dhammaṃ saṅghañ ca tādinaṃ
samādiyāhi sīlāni taṃ te atthāya hehiti.[3]

250 upemi saraṇaṃ buddhaṃ dhammaṃ saṅghañ ca tādinaṃ
samādiyāmi sīlāni taṃ me atthāya hehiti.

251 brahmabandhu pure āsiṃ ajjamhi saccabrāhmaṇo
tevijjo vedasampanno sottiyo camhi nhātako ti.[4]

Good lady, I give you this shawl 246
that covered me when I washed in water,
let it be yours, I don't want it.

Punna

If you fear suffering, if you dislike suffering, 247
don't do action that is evil, whether openly or in secret.

If you will do action that is evil, 248
or already did it,
you won't be freed from the suffering that comes to you,
even if you jump up and run away.

If you fear suffering, if you dislike suffering, 249
take refuge in the Buddha, the dhamma that he taught,
and the sangha that has qualities like his,
develop your moral virtues, that will be for your benefit.

The Brahman

I take refuge in the Buddha, the dhamma that he taught, 250
and the sangha that has qualities like his,
I will develop my moral virtues, it will be for my benefit.

I may have been born in a Brahman family, 251
but now I really am a Brahman,
I know the three things that most don't know,[2]
I am learned, I have attained the highest knowledge,
I am washed clean.[3]

vīsatinipāto

ambapālī

252 kāḷakā bhamaravaṇṇasādisā vellitaggā mama muddhajā
ahuṃ
te jarāya sāṇavākasādisā saccavādivacanaṃ anaññathā.

253 vāsito va surabhī karaṇḍako pupphapūra mama
uttamaṅgajo[1]
taṃ jarāya sasalomagandhikaṃ[2] saccavādivacanaṃ
anaññathā.

254 kānanaṃ va sahitaṃ suropitaṃ
kocchasūcivicitaggasobhitaṃ
taṃ jarāya viralaṃ tahiṃ tahiṃ saccavādivacanaṃ
anaññathā.

POEMS WITH ABOUT TWENTY VERSES

Ambapali

The[1] hairs on my head were once curly, 252
black, like the color of bees,
now because of old age
they are like jute.

It's just as the Buddha, the speaker of truth, said,
nothing different than that.

The hair on my head was[2] once scented 253
like a perfumed box filled with flowers,
now because of old age
it smells like rabbit fur.

It's just as the Buddha, the speaker of truth, said,
nothing different than that.

It was beautiful the way it was held in bunches by pins 254
like a thick and well-planted forest grove,
now because of old age
it is sparse in many spots.

255 kaṇhakhandhakasuvaṇṇamaṇḍitaṃ[3] sobhate taṃ su
veṇīhilaṅkataṃ
taṃ jarāya khalitaṃ siraṃ kataṃ saccavādivacanaṃ
anaññathā.

256 cittakārasukatā va lekhikā sobhate subhamukā pure mama
tā jarāya valīhi palambitā saccavādivacanaṃ anaññathā.

257 bhassarā surucirā yathā maṇī nettahesum abhinīlamāyatā
te jarāyabhihatā na sobhate saccavādivacanaṃ anaññathā.

It's just as the Buddha, the speaker of truth, said,
nothing different than that.

My head was beautiful, decorated with braids, 255
adorned with gold amid the masses of black,
now because of old age
it has become bald.

It's just as the Buddha, the speaker of truth, said,
nothing different than that.

Once my eyebrows were beautiful 256
like the contour lines drawn first by a good artist,
now because of old age
they are bent out of shape by wrinkles.

It's just as the Buddha, the speaker of truth, said,
nothing different than that.

My eyes were black and innocent,[3] 257
like jewels that are beautiful and brilliant,
now struck by old age, they do not shine.

It's just as the Buddha, the speaker of truth, said,
nothing different than that.

258 saṇhatuṅgasadisī ca nāsikā sobhate su abhiyobbanaṃ pati
sā jarāya upakūlitā viya saccavādivacanaṃ anaññathā.

259 kaṅkaṇaṃ va sukataṃ suniṭṭhitaṃ sobhate su mama
kaṇṇapāḷiyo
tā jarāya valihi palambitā saccavādivacanaṃ anaññathā.

260 pattalīmakulavaṇṇasādisā sobhate su dantā pure mama
te jarāya khaṇḍitā ca pitakā saccavādivacanaṃ[4] anaññathā.

When I was young, my nose was beautiful, 258
it was delicate, high, and was perfect for my face,[4]
now because of old age
it is like a strip of wet leather.[5]

It's just as the Buddha, the speaker of truth, said,
nothing different than that.

My earlobes were beautiful 259
like well-crafted bracelets, finished to perfection,
now because of old age
they are bent out of shape by wrinkles.

It's just as the Buddha, the speaker of truth, said,
nothing different than that.

Once my teeth were beautiful, 260
they looked like plantain buds,
now because of old age,
they are broken and yellow.

It's just as the Buddha, the speaker of truth, said,
nothing different than that.

261 kānanamhi vanasaṇḍacārinī kokilā va madhuraṃ
    nikūjihaṃ[5]
tаṃ jarāya khalitaṃ tahiṃ tahiṃ saccavādivacanaṃ
    anaññathā.

262 saṇhakamburiva suppamajjitā sobhate va sugīvā pure
    mama
sā jarāya bhaggā vināmitā saccavādivacanaṃ anaññathā.

263 vaṭṭapalighasadisopamā ubho sobhate subāhā pure mama
tā jarāya yathā pāṭalippalitā[6] saccavādivacanaṃ
    anaññathā.

Once I could sing sweetly 261
like a cuckoo about in a dense forest,
now because of old age
at times my voice cracks.

It's just as the Buddha, the speaker of truth, said,
nothing different than that.

Once my neck was beautiful 262
like a polished and smooth conchshell,
now because of old age
it is bent and misshapen.

It's just as the Buddha, the speaker of truth, said,
nothing different than that.

Once my arms were both beautiful 263
like the round iron crossbars for holding doors shut,
now because of old age
they are gray like the bark of the *patali* tree.[6]

It's just as the Buddha, the speaker of truth, said,
nothing different than that.

264 saṇhamuddikasuvaṇṇamaṇḍitā sobhate suhatthā pure mama
te jarāya yathā mūlamūlikā saccavādivacanaṃ anaññathā.

265 pīnavaṭṭasahituggatā ubho sobhate suthanakā pure mama
thevikī va[7] lambanti nodakā saccavādivacanaṃ anaññathā.

266 kañcanassa phalakaṃ va sammaṭṭhaṃ sobhate sukāyo pure mama
so valīhi sukhumāhi otato saccavādivacanaṃ anaññathā.

Once my hands were both beautiful, 264
decorated with smooth rings made of gold,
now because of old age,
they are like tree-roots and root-vegetables.

It's just as the Buddha, the speaker of truth, said,
nothing different than that.

Once my breasts were beautiful, 265
full, round, close together, high,
now they sag down,
like empty waterbags made of leather.[7]

It's just as the Buddha, the speaker of truth, said,
nothing different than that.

Once my body was beautiful, 266
like a polished slab of gold,
now it is covered
with very fine wrinkles.

It's just as the Buddha, the speaker of truth, said,
nothing different than that.

267 nāgabhogasadisopamā ubho sobhate suūrū pure mama
te jarāya yathā veḷunāḷiyo saccavādivacanaṃ anaññathā.

268 saṇhanūpurasuvaṇṇamaṇḍitā sobhate sujaṅghā pure mama
tā jarāya tiladaṇḍakāriva saccavādivacanaṃ anaññathā.

269 tūlapuṇṇasadisopamā ubho sobhate supādā pure mama
te jarāya phuṭitā valīmatā saccavādivacanaṃ anaññathā.

Once my thighs were beautiful, 267
like the trunk of an elephant,
now because of old age,
they are bamboo sticks.

It's just as the Buddha, the speaker of truth, said,
nothing different than that.

Once my calves were beautiful, 268
decorated with smooth anklets made of gold,
now because of old age,
they are like sesame switches.

It's just as the Buddha, the speaker of truth, said,
nothing different than that.

Once my feet were beautiful, 269
so soft they seemed filled with cotton,
now because of old age
they are wrinkled, with calluses cracked.

It's just as the Buddha, the speaker of truth, said,
nothing different than that.

270 īdiso ahu ayaṃ samussayo jajjaro bahudukkhānam ālayo
sopalepapatito jarāgharo saccavādivacanaṃ anaññathā ti.

rohinī

271 samaṇā ti bhoti tvaṃ sayasi samaṇā ti paṭibujjhasi
samaṇānam eva kittesi samaṇī nūna bhavissasi.

272 vipulaṃ annañ ca pānañ ca samaṇānaṃ payacchasi
rohinī dāni pucchāmi kena te samaṇā piyā.

273 akammakāmā alasā paradatto pajīvino
āsaṃsukā sādukāmā kena te samaṇā piyā.

This body was once like that, 270
now feeble with age and fallen from its pride,
it is the home of many sufferings,
like an old house, the plaster falling down.[8]

It's just as the Buddha, the speaker of truth, said,
nothing different than that.

Rohini

Repeating at the time of her enlightenment what her father once said to her

Good[9] lady, you fell asleep saying, "ascetics," 271
you woke up saying the same,
you give praise only to ascetics,
it must be that is what you are planning to become.

You give a lot of food and drink to ascetics, 272
Rohini, now I ask you,
what is the reason why
ascetics are so dear to you?

They don't like to work, they're lazy, 273
living on what is given by others,
full of expectations, liking sweet things,
so just what is the reason why
ascetics are so dear to you?

274 cirassaṃ vata maṃ tāta samaṇānaṃ paripucchasi
tesaṃ te kittayissāmi paññāsīlaparakkamaṃ.

275 kammakāmā analasā kammaseṭṭhassa kārakā
rāgaṃ dosaṃ pajahanti tena me samaṇā piyā.

276 tīṇi pāpassa mūlāni dhunanti sucikārino
sabbapāpaṃ pahīnesaṃ tena me samaṇā piyā.

277 kāyakammaṃ suci nesaṃ vacīkammañ ca tādisaṃ
manokammaṃ suci nesaṃ tena me samaṇā piyā.

278 vimalā saṅkhamuttā va suddhā santarabāhirā
puṇṇā sukkehi dhammehi tena me samaṇā piyā.

Remembering what she replied

You have been asking me about ascetics 274
for a long time, father,
I will praise them to you,
their wisdom, their virtue, and their effort.

They do like to work, they're not lazy, 275
they do the best kinds of actions,
that's how they get rid of passion and anger—
and that is the reason why
ascetics are so dear to me.

They have destroyed the three roots of evil,[10] 276
they do what is pure,
all evil is expelled for them—
that is the reason why
ascetics are so dear to me.

What they do with their bodies is pure, 277
and it is the same with what they say,
even what they think is pure—
that is the reason why
ascetics are so dear to me.

Spotless like mother of pearl or like a pearl itself, 278
pure inside and out,
filled with bright things[11]—
that is the reason why
ascetics are so dear to me.

279 bahussutā dhammadharā ariyā dhammajīvino
atthaṃ dhammañ ca desenti tena me samaṇā piyā.

280 bahussutā dhammadharā ariyā dhammajīvino
ekaggacittā satimanto tena me samaṇā piyā.

281 dūraṅgamā satimanto mantabhāṇī anuddhatā
dukkhassantaṃ pajānanti tena me samaṇā piyā.

282 yasmā gāmā pakkamanti na vilokenti kiñcanaṃ
anapekkhā va gacchanti tena me samaṇā piyā.

283 na tesaṃ koṭṭhe openti na kumbhiṃ na khalopiyaṃ
pariniṭṭhitam esānā tena me samaṇā piyā.

Learned, they know what the Buddha taught by heart, 279
they teach his dhamma and its purpose—
that is the reason why
ascetics are so dear to me.

Learned, they know what the Buddha taught by heart, 280
noble, they live what the Buddha taught,
minds focused, mindful—
that is the reason why
ascetics are so dear to me.

They travel far, ever mindful, 281
reciting words of wisdom, subdued,
they know for themselves the end of suffering—
that is the reason why
ascetics are so dear to me.

Whatever village they may leave, 282
they do not look back with any attachment,
without any longing, they go on—
that is the reason why
ascetics are so dear to me.

They do not save anything that is theirs 283
in a storeroom or in a pot or a container,
searching instead for what is already prepared[12]—
that is the reason why
ascetics are so dear to me.

284 na te hiraññaṃ gaṇhanti na suvaṇṇaṃ na rūpiyaṃ
paccuppannena yāpenti tena me samaṇā piyā.

285 nānākulā pabbajitā nānājanapadehi ca
aññamaññaṃ piyāyanti tena me samaṇā piyā.

286 atthāya vata no bhoti kule jātāsi rohinī
saddhā buddhe ca dhamme ca saṅghe ca tibbagāravā.

287 tuvaṃ hetaṃ pajānāsi puññakkhettaṃ anuttaraṃ
amham pi ca te samaṇā paṭigaṇhanti dakkhiṇaṃ.[8]

288 patiṭṭhito hettha yañño vipulo no bhavissati
sace bhāyasi dukkhassa sace te dukkham appiyaṃ.[9]

They do not take gold 284
or gold coins or silver,
they get by with whatever is available—
that is the reason why
ascetics are so dear to me.

Those who have gone forth 285
are from various families and from various regions
and still they are friendly with each other—
that is the reason why
ascetics are so dear to me.

Repeating what her father then said to her

Rohini, my dear, I can see 286
that you were born in our family for a reason,
you have faith in the Buddha,
and you are very devoted to his dhamma
and his sangha.

You understand that his community 287
is a great field for the making of merit,
so let these ascetics take our gift as well.

If you fear suffering, 288
if you dislike suffering,
any offering that is made
will have extensive consequences.

289 upehi saraṇaṃ buddhaṃ dhammaṃ saṅghañ ca tādinaṃ
samādiyāhi sīlāni taṃ te atthāya hehiti.

290 upemi saraṇaṃ buddhaṃ dhammaṃ saṅghañ ca tādinaṃ
samādiyāmi sīlāni taṃ me atthāya hehiti.

291 brahmabandhu pure āsiṃ so idānimhi brāhmaṇo
tevijjo sottiyo camhi vedagū camhi nhātako ti.

cāpā

292 laṭṭhihattho pure āsi so dāni migaluddako
āsāya palipā ghorā nāsakkhi pārametave.

Repeating what she said to her father

Take refuge in the Buddha, the dhamma that he taught, 289
and the sangha that has qualities like his,
develop your moral virtues, that will be for your benefit.

Repeating what her father said

I take refuge in the Buddha, the dhamma that he taught, 290
and the sangha that has qualities like his,
I will develop my moral virtues, it will be for my benefit.

I may have been born in a Brahman family, 291
but it's only now that I really am a Brahman,
I have the three knowledges, I am learned,
I have attained the highest knowledge,
I am washed clean.

Chapa

Repeating at the time of her enlightenment a dialogue

Chapa's husband

In[13] the past 292
wasn't it me who carried an ascetic's staff?
Now I am a deer-hunter,
unable to get out of this foul mud
and reach the other shore
because of desire.

293 sumattaṃ maṃ maññamā nā cā pā puttam atosayi
cāpāya bandhanaṃ chetvā pabbajissaṃ puno cahaṃ.

294 mā me kujjhi mahāvīra mā me kujjhi mahāmuni
na hi kodhaparetassa suddhi atthi kuto tapo.

295 pakkamissañ ca nālāto kodha nālāya vacchati
bandhantī itthirūpena samaṇe dhammajīvino.

296 ehi kāla nivattassu bhuñja kāme yathā pure
ahañ ca te vasīkatā ye ca me santi ñātakā.

Confident that I would remain infatuated, 293
my wife gave all her attention to our son, to make him
happy,
but once I cut my tie to her
I will renounce again.

Chapa

Please don't be angry with me, big man, 294
great sage, don't get mad.
There is no purity of mind
for one overcome by anger.
From where will self-control come?

Chapa's husband

I will leave Nala, 295
who can live here in Nala?
Virtuous ascetics get trapped
by the physical beauties of women.

Chapa

Come here, good-looking, just stay, 296
enjoy whatever you want
like you used to with me,
I will be at your command,
and so will my relatives.

297 etto cāpe catubbhāgaṃ yathā bhāsasi tvañ ca me
tayi rattassa posassa ulāraṃ vata taṃ siyā.

298 kāḷaṅginiṃ va takkāriṃ pupphitaṃ girimuddhani
phullaṃ dāḷimalaṭṭhiṃ va antodīpeva pāṭaliṃ.

299 haricandanalittaṅgiṃ kāsikuttamadhāriniṃ
taṃ maṃ rūpavatiṃ santiṃ kassa ohāya gacchasi.

300 sākuntiko va sakuṇiṃ yathā bandhitum icchati
āharimena rūpena na maṃ tvaṃ bādhayissasi.

Chapa's husband

Chapa, if there were only one-quarter 297
of what you just said
that would be more than enough
for any man in love with you.

Chapa

Good-looking, that body of yours 298
is like a *takkarim* tree on top of a mountain
gorgeous in full bloom,
it's like a blooming *dalima* vine
or like a *patali* tree
standing up straight in the middle of an island.

If you go, leaving me behind, 299
who will physically enjoy this body of mine
adorned with sandalwood,
covered with the best cloths from Kasi?[14]

Chapa's husband

You want to catch me, 300
like the fowler with his snares for birds.
You will not trap me
with your fetching body.

301 imañ ca me puttaphalaṃ kāḷa uppāditaṃ tayā
taṃ maṃ puttavatiṃ santiṃ kassa ohāya gacchasi.

302 jahanti putte sappaññā tato ñātī tato dhanaṃ
pabbajanti mahā vīrā nāgo chetvā va bandhanaṃ.

303 idāni te imaṃ puttaṃ daṇḍena churikāya vā
bhūmiyaṃ vā nisumbhissaṃ puttasokā na gacchasi.

304 sace puttaṃ siṅgālānaṃ kukkurānaṃ padāhisi
na maṃ puttakatte jammi punar āvattayissasi.

Chapa

And, good-looking, what about this child, 301
born because of you?
Who are you leaving
when you leave me,
the one who has this child?

Chapa's husband

Those who are wise 302
leave behind children,
relatives, and wealth,
great ascetics renounce the world
like an elephant breaking its tether.

Chapa

I shall knock this son of yours 303
flat to the ground,
use a stick or a knife on him,
and then from grief for the child
you won't go.

Chapa's husband

Even if you give that child 304
to jackals or dogs,
you will not make me turn around,
you wretched baby-maker.

305 handa kho dāni bhaddante kuhiṃ kāḷa gamissasi
katamaṃ gāmaṃ nigamaṃ nagaraṃ rājadhāniyo.

306 ahumha pubbe gaṇino assamaṇā samaṇamānino
gāmena gāmaṃ vicarimha nagare rājadhāniyo.

307 eso hi bhagavā buddho nadiṃ nerañjaraṃ pati
sabbadukkhappahānāya dhammaṃ deseti pāṇinaṃ.

308 tassāhaṃ santikaṃ gacchaṃ so me satthā bhavissati
vandanaṃ dāni vajjāsi lokanāthaṃ anuttaraṃ.

309 padakkhiṇañ ca katvāna ādiseyyāsi dakkhiṇaṃ
etaṃ kho labbham amhehi yathā bhāsasi tvañ ca me.

Chapa

Good luck to you then, good-looking, 305
but where will you go,
to what village or town,
to what city or capital?

Chapa's husband

Once I was a leader of others, 306
all proud that we were ascetics
even when we really weren't,
we went from town to town,
to cities and to the capital.

The Lord, the Buddha is near 307
right by the Neranjara River,
where he is teaching the dhamma
that leads to the ending of all suffering
for all beings.

I will go to where he is 308
and he will be my teacher.
You too should speak praise
about the supreme lord of the world.

And you too should honor him by circling around him, 309
and give him the gift that he is due
This is what is possible for us—
say it is so, for both you and me.

310 vandanaṃ dāni te vajjaṃ lokanāthaṃ anuttaraṃ
padakkhiṇañ ca katvāna ādisissāmi dakkhiṇaṃ.

311 tato ca kāḷo pakkāmi nadiṃ nerañjaraṃ pati
so addasāsi sambuddhaṃ desentaṃ amataṃ padaṃ.

312 dukkhaṃ dukkhasamuppādaṃ dukkhassa ca atikkamaṃ
ariyaṃ caṭṭhaṅgikaṃ maggaṃ dukkhūpasamagāminaṃ.

313 tassa pādāni vanditvā katvā na naṃ padakkhiṇaṃ
cāpāya ādisitvāna pabbajiṃ anagāriyaṃ
tisso vijjā anuppattā kataṃ buddhassa sāsanan ti.

Chapa

I too shall speak praise 310
about the supreme lord of the world,
and having honored him by circumambulating
I will give him the gift that is due.

Those who compiled the Scriptures said

And so her handsome husband left 311
for the Neranjara River,
where he saw the Buddha teaching
about the deathless place that is as sweet as nectar,[15]

about suffering and its arising, 312
about the overcoming of suffering,
and the noble eightfold path
that ends with suffering ended.[16]

Having worshiped his feet 313
and circumambulated,
he dedicated the merit[17] to Chapa
and went forth to the homeless state.
He knows the three things that most don't know,[18]
what the Buddha taught is done.

sundarī

314 petāni bhoti puttāni khādamānā tuvaṃ pure
tuvaṃ divā ca ratto ca atīva paritappasi.

315 sājja sabbāni khāditvā sataputtāni[10] brāhmaṇī
vāseṭṭhi kena vaṇṇena na bāḷhaṃ paritappasi.

316 bahūni puttasatāni ñātisaṅghasatāni ca
khāditāni atītaṃse mama tuyhañ ca brāhmaṇa.

317 sāhaṃ nissaraṇaṃ ñatvā jātiyā maraṇassa ca
na socāmi na rodāmi na cāpi paritappayiṃ.

318 abbhutaṃ vata vāseṭṭhi vācaṃ bhāsasi edisiṃ
kassa tvaṃ dhammam aññāya giraṃ bhāsasi edisiṃ.

Sundari

Repeating at the time of her enlightenment a dialogue

Sundari's father

My[19] lady, in the past people called you 314
someone who ate her dead sons,[20]
still you grieved hard for them day and night.

Today, Brahman lady, although you have eaten 315
hundreds of children,
why, Vasetthi, don't you grieve so much?[21]

Vasetthi's reply to her father

Many hundreds of sons, 316
as well as hundreds of relatives,
mine as well as yours
were eaten in the past, Brahman.

Now that I know the way to leave birth and death behind, 317
I do not mourn nor do I cry,
And I no longer grieve.

Sundari's father

What you say is truly amazing, Vasetthi; 318
who taught you his dhamma
that you can say something as inspired as this?

319 esa brāhmaṇa sambuddho nagaraṃ mithilaṃ pati
sabbadukkhappahānāya dhammaṃ desesi pāṇinaṃ.

320 tassa brahmaṇa arahato dhammaṃ sutvā nirūpadhiṃ
tattha viññātasaddhammā puttasokaṃ vyapānudiṃ.

321 so aham pi gamissāmi nagaraṃ mithilaṃ pati
appeva maṃ so bhagavā sabbadukkhā pamocaye.

322 addasa brāhmaṇo buddhaṃ vippamuttaṃ nirūpadhiṃ
sossa dhammam adesesi muni dukkhassa pāragū.

323 dukkhaṃ dukkhasamuppādaṃ dukkhassa ca atikkamaṃ
ariyaṃ caṭṭhaṅgikaṃ maggaṃ dukkhūpasamagāminaṃ.

Vasetthi

The Buddha is near Mithila city, Brahman, 319
there he is teaching the dhamma
that leads to the ending of all suffering
for all beings.

I have heard the dhamma from that worthy one, 320
the truth that is free from all that holds us back,
and as soon as that dhamma was known,
I could drive away my grief for lost children.

Sundari's father

I too will go to that place near Mithila, 321
I hope that Bhagavan[22] will free me
from all suffering too.

Those who compiled the Scriptures said

The Brahman saw the Buddha, 322
saw that he was free and would not be reborn,
and that sage who had gone beyond suffering
taught the dhamma to him,

he taught about suffering, 323
how suffering comes to be,
and how one goes beyond it,
he taught the noble eightfold path
that goes to the stilling of suffering.[23]

324 tattha viññātasaddhammo pabbajjaṃ samarocayi[11]
sujāto tīhi rattīhi tisso vijjā aphassayi.

325 ehi sārathi gacchāhi rathaṃ nīyādayāhimaṃ
ārogyaṃ brāhmaṇiṃ vajja pabbajito dāni brāhmaṇo
sujāto tīhi rattīhi tisso vijjā aphassayi.[12]

326 tato ca ratham ādāya sahassaṃ cāpi sārathi
ārogyaṃ brāhmaṇiṃ voca pabbajito dāni brāhmaṇo
sujāto tīhi rattīhi tisso vijjā aphassayi.

327 etaṃ cahaṃ assarathaṃ sahassaṃ cāpi sārathi
tevijjaṃ brāhmaṇaṃ sutvā puṇṇapattaṃ dadāmi te.

The moment that dhamma was known 324
he found delight in going forth,
and after three nights,
Sujata[24] knew the three things
that most don't know.[25]

Sundari's father

Come, driver,[26] take this chariot and go, 325
convey my wishes for her good health to my wife
but tell her that I have gone forth,
and that I knew the three things
that most don't know[27] after three nights.

Spoken by those who compiled the Scriptures

The driver took the chariot and a thousand coins, 326
he gave the message to the Brahman woman
about her husband's wishes for her health,
that Sujata had gone forth,
and that he knew the three things
that most don't know after three nights.

Sundari's mother

Just hearing that my husband knows 327
the three things that most don't know,
I feel like I have a full bowl to give,
And so, driver,
I give you this horse and chariot and the thousand coins.

328 tumheva hotu assaratho sahassañ cā pi brāhmaṇi
aham pi pabbajissāmi varapaññassa santike.

329 hatthī gavassaṃ maṇikuṇḍalañ ca phītaṃ cimaṃ
gahavibhavaṃ pahāya
pitā pabbajito tuyhaṃ bhuñja bhogāni sundari tuvaṃ
dāyādikā kule.

330 hatthī gavassaṃ maṇikuṇḍalañ ca rammaṃ cimaṃ
gahavibhavaṃ pahāya
pitā pabbajito mayhaṃ puttasokena aṭṭito
aham pi pabbajissāmi bhātu sokena aṭṭitā.

331 so te ijjhatu saṅkappo yaṃ tvaṃ patthesi sundari
uttiṭṭhapiṇḍo uñcho ca paṃsukūlaṃ ca cīvaraṃ
etāni abhisambhontī paraloke anāsavā.

The charioteer

Brahman lady, you can keep the horse and chariot 328
the thousand coins too,
I too will go forth
in the presence of him who has the best wisdom.

Sundari's mother

Sundari, your father has gone forth 329
leaving behind elephants, cows, and horses,
jewels and earrings, and all the riches of this house.
You are the heir in the family, now you can enjoy this
wealth.

Sundari

My father has gone forth 330
leaving behind elephants, cows, and horses,
jewels and earrings, and all the riches of this house,
because he was oppressed by grief for his son,
and I too will go forth, because I am oppressed
by grief for my brother as well.

Sundari's mother

May it all turn out as you wish, Sundari, 331
but there will be picking up as alms what others discard
and wearing rags as a robe.
If you can be happy with such things,
in the next world, you will be free
from all that defiles from within.

332 sikkhamānāya me ayye dibbacakkhu visodhitaṃ
pubbenivāsaṃ jānāmi yattha me vusitaṃ pure.

333 tuvaṃ nissāya kalyāṇī therī saṅghassa[13] sobhane
tisso vijjā anuppattā kataṃ buddhassa sāsanaṃ.

334 anujānāhi me ayye icche sāvatthi gantave
sīhanādaṃ nadissāmi buddhaseṭṭhassa santike.

335 passa sundari satthāraṃ hemavaṇṇaṃ harittacaṃ
adantānaṃ dametāraṃ sambuddham akutobhayaṃ.

336 passa sundarim āyantiṃ vippamuttaṃ nirūpadhiṃ
vītarāgaṃ visaṃyuttaṃ katakiccam anāsavaṃ.

Sundari speaking to her preceptor

The eye that sees the invisible 332
I have cleansed through training,
I know my previous lives, honored one,
I know where I have lived before.

By relying on you, beautiful *therī,* 333
you who are an ornament to the sangha.
I know the three things that most don't know,[28]
what the Buddha taught is done.

Give me permission, honored one, to go to Savatthi, 334
I will roar like a lion[29] in the presence of the Buddha.

Sundari speaking to herself as she approaches the Buddha in Savatthi

Look at the teacher, Sundari, 335
he is the color of gold, his skin is all golden,
the Buddha is the tamer of those untamed,
afraid of no one and nothing.

May the Buddha see me coming toward him, 336
see that I am completely free, free from all that holds us back,
passion gone, set free, what needs to be done done,
free from all that defiles from within.

337 bārāṇasīto nikkhamma tava santikam āgatā
sāvikā te mahāvīra pāde vandati sundarī.

338 tuvaṃ buddho tuvaṃ satthā tuyhaṃ dhītamhi brāhmaṇa
orasā mukhato jātā katakiccā anāsavā.

339 tassā te svāgataṃ bhadde tato te adurāgataṃ
evaṃ hi dantā āyanti satthu pādāni vandikā
vītarāgā visaṃyuttā katakiccā anāsavā ti.

subhā kammāradhītā

340 daharāhaṃ suddhavasanā yaṃ pure dhammam assuṇiṃ
tassā me appamattāya saccābhisamayo ahu.

Sundari to the Buddha

Sundari is your disciple, Great Hero, 337
she left Benares and came to where you are,
and now she bows to your feet.

You are the Buddha, you are my teacher, 338
Brahman,[30] I am your daughter,
your own child, born from your mouth,
all that needs to be done has been done,
I am free from all that defiles from within.

Spoken by the Buddha to Sundari

Fortunate lady, you are welcome here, 339
this is where you belong,
the same as those who have tamed themselves,
whose passion is gone, who are set free,
who have done what needs to be done
and are free from all that defiles from within,
who all come and bow to the feet of the teacher.

Subha, the metalworker's daughter

I[31] first heard the Buddha's dhamma when I was still young, 340
it was on a day when I was wearing clean clothes,
and by my own effort,
there was comprehension of the four noble truths.

341 tatohaṃ sabbakāmesu bhusaṃ aratim ajjhagaṃ
sakkāyasmiṃ bhayaṃ disvā nekkhammaññeva pīhaye.

342 hitvānahaṃ ñātigaṇaṃ dāsakammakarāni ca
gāmakhettāni phītāni ramaṇīye pamodite.

343 pahāyahaṃ pabbajitā sāpateyyam anappakaṃ
evaṃ saddhāya nikkhamma saddhamme suppavedite.

344 na me taṃ assa patirūpaṃ ākiñcaññaṃ hi patthaye
yo jātarūpaṃ rajataṃ chaḍḍetvā[14] punar āgame.[15]

345 rajataṃ jātarūpaṃ vā na bodhāya na santiyā
netaṃ samaṇasāruppaṃ na etaṃ ariyaṃ dhanaṃ.

346 lobhanaṃ madanaṃ cetaṃ mohanaṃ rajavaḍḍhanaṃ
sāsaṅkaṃ bahu āyāsaṃ natthi cettha dhuvaṃ ṭhiti.

Right then I found that I had 341
a great dislike for all that my senses find pleasing,
I was afraid of my own body,
and I longed for freedom from it all.

I left my relatives, slaves, and workers, 342
the rich villages and their fields,
everything pleasing and delightful,

I left more than a little wealth, I went forth, 343
I went forward, with my faith like that,
into the dhamma that had been so well-taught.

So it is not right for me now, 344
when I desire nothing at all,
to come back again
to the silver and gold I have thrown away.

Silver and gold don't lead 345
to awakening and peace,
they are not fit for an ascetic,
they are a wealth that is not noble.

Wealth comes with greediness, makes your head spin, 346
it deludes and it increases defilements,
it brings many sorrows and is dangerous,
there is nothing you can count on with wealth.

347 ettha rattā pamattā ca saṃkiliṭṭhamanā narā
aññamaññena vyāruddhā puthu kubbanti medhagaṃ.

348 vadho bandho parikleso jāni sokapariddavo
kāmesu adhipannānaṃ dissate vyasanaṃ bahuṃ.

349 taṃ maṃ ñātī amittā va kiṃ vo kāmesu yuñjatha
jānātha maṃ pabbajitaṃ kāmesu bhayadassiniṃ.

350 na hiraññasuvaṇṇena parikkhīyanti āsavā
amittā vadhakā kāmā sapattā sallabandhanā.

351 taṃ maṃ ñātī amittā va kiṃ vo kāmesu yuñjatha
jānātha maṃ pabbajitaṃ muṇḍaṃ saṅghāṭipārutaṃ.

352 uttiṭṭhapiṇḍo uñcho ca paṃsukūlaṃ ca cīvaraṃ
etaṃ kho mama sāruppaṃ anagārūpanissayo.

Men get excited near wealth, and they get careless too, 347
their minds become dirty,
wealth makes them ever at odds with each other,
and they endlessly fight among themselves.

Death and bondage, calamity and robbery, 348
grief and lamentation—there are so many miseries
for those who get caught among what pleases the senses.

My relatives, you know that I have gone forth, 349
that I have seen what is fearful in what pleases the senses
so why are you trying to get me to go back to those
    pleasures
as if you were my enemies?

Gold and money do not lessen 350
the depravities that ooze out from within,
urges that come from our senses are enemies,
butchers, foes who bind us with ropes.

My relatives, you know that I have gone forth, 351
that my head is shaven and I wear a nun's robe,
so why are you trying to get me to go back to those
    pleasures
as if you were my enemies?

Picking up as alms what others discard 352
and wearing rags as a robe,
that is what suits me,
it is all that is needed for someone homeless.

353 vantā mahesīhi kāmā ye dibbā ye ca mānusā
khemaṭṭhāne vimuttā te pattā te acalaṃ sukhaṃ.

354 nāhaṃ kāmehi saṅgacchiṃ yesu tāṇaṃ na vijjati
amittā vadhakā kāmā aggikkhandhasamā[16] dukhā.

355 paripantho esa bhayo[17] savighāto sakaṇṭako
gedho suvisamo lopo[18] mahanto mohanāmukho.

356 upasaggo bhīmarūpo kāmā sappasirūpamā
ye bālā abhinandanti andhabhūtā puthujjanā.

357 kāmapaṅkena sattā hi bahū loke aviddasū
pariyantaṃ nābhijānanti jātiyā maraṇassa ca.

358 duggatigamanaṃ maggaṃ manussā kāmahetukaṃ
bahuṃ ve paṭipajjanti attano rogam āvahaṃ.

Great sages have given up all pleasures of the senses, 353
divine and human pleasures,
they are free, in the place of peace,
they have attained constant happiness.

Let me not even find something that pleases the senses, 354
no place of safety exists among them,
they are enemies, butchers,
the sufferings they bring do what large fires do.

Greed is dangerous, fearful, 355
destructive, it has thorns,
it is so very wrong, harmful too,
it makes one stupid.

The urges that come from the senses are trouble, 356
they are frightening, like a snake's head,
yet ordinary people, always blind, ever fools,
are still delighted by them.

Many people in the world are really fools. 357
Because of the mud of what pleases the senses,
they have no idea where the bounds of birth and death are.

On account of the urges of the senses, 358
humans happily follow the road
to lives of misery,[32]
they bring sickness on themselves.

359 evaṃ amittajananā tāpanā saṃkilesikā
lokāmisā bandhanīyā kāmā caraṇabandhanā.[19]

360 ummādanā ullapanā kāmā cittappamāthino[20]
sattānaṃ saṅkilesāya khipaṃ[21] mārena oḍḍitaṃ.

361 anantādīnavā kāmā bahudukkhā mahāvisā
appassādā raṇakarā sukkapakkhavisosakā.[22]

362 sāhaṃ etādisaṃ katvā vyasanaṃ kāmahetukaṃ
na taṃ paccāgamissāmi nibbānābhiratā sadā.

363 raṇaṃ karitvā kāmānaṃ sītibhāvābhikaṅkhinī
appamattā vihassāmi[23] tesaṃ saṃyojanakkhaye.

364 asokaṃ virajaṃ khemaṃ ariyañ caṭṭhaṅgikaṃ ujuṃ
taṃ maggaṃ anugacchāmi yena tiṇṇā mahesino.

That's how the urges of the senses give us enemies, 359
they are burning and defiling,
the bait in the snare of the world,
fetters, shackles to our actions.

The urges of the senses are maddening, enticing, 360
they trouble the mind, they are
a net laid out as a trap by Mara
to defile beings.

The urges of the senses are endless dangers, 361
they bring many kinds of suffering and are a great poison,
they give little satisfaction, and instead bring grief,
they dry up the good opportunities that come.[33]

On account of the urges of the senses, 362
I have ruined so much.
I will not go back to that again,
now I always take my delight in nibbana.

Longing to become cool, 363
I did battle with the urges of the senses.
I will live diligent
while the shackles of those urges pass away.

I will go on that path 364
by which great sages have reached nibbana.
It is griefless, faultless, full of peace, straight,
the noble eightfold path.

365 imaṃ passatha dhammaṭṭhaṃ subhaṃ kammāradhītaraṃ
anejaṃ upasampajja rukkhamūlamhi jhāyati.

366 ajjaṭṭhamī pabbajitā saddhā saddhammasobhanā
vinītuppalavaṇṇāya tevijjā maccuhāyinī.

367 sāyaṃ bhujissā anaṇā bhikkhunī bhāvitindriyā
sabbayogavisaṃyuttā katakiccā anāsavā.

368 taṃ sakko devasaṅghena upasaṅkamma iddhiyā
namassati bhūtapati subhaṃ kammāradhītaran ti.

Spoken by the Buddha to praise Subha

Look at Subha, the metalworker's daughter, 365
she has become calm,
she meditates at the foot of a tree.

Today is the eighth day since she went forth, faithful, 366
she is beautiful[34] because she has realized dhamma,
taught by Uppalavanna, she knows
the three things that most don't know[35]
and she has left death behind.

Subha is a slave who has been freed, she now has no debt, 367
a nun who knows how to know well,
free from everything that held her back,
she has done what needs to be done
and is free from the depravities that ooze out from within.

Those who compiled the Scriptures said

Sakka, the lord of beings, used his powers 368
to come with a host of gods,
and he worshiped Subha, the metalworker's daughter.

tiṃsanipāto

subhā jīvakambavanikā

369 jīvakambavanaṃ rammaṃ gacchantiṃ bhikkhuniṃ subhaṃ
dhuttako sannivāresi tam enaṃ abravī subhā.

370 kiṃ te aparādhitaṃ mayā yaṃ maṃ ovariyāna tiṭṭhasi
na hi pabbajitāya āvuso puriso samphusanāya kappati.

371 garuke mama satthu sāsane yā sikkhā sugatena desitā
parisuddhapadaṃ anaṅgaṇaṃ kiṃ maṃ ovariyāna tiṭṭhasi.

372 āvilacitto anāvilaṃ sarajo vītarajaṃ anaṅgaṇaṃ
sabbattha vimuttamānasaṃ kiṃ maṃ ovariyāna tiṭṭhasi.

A POEM WITH ABOUT THIRTY VERSES

Subha of the Jivakamba Grove

As[1] the nun Subha entered the beautiful Jivakamba Grove 369
a rake grabbed her and Subha said this to him:

Subha

Friend, it is not right for a man 370
to touch a woman who has gone forth,
why do you keep me from my way?

I am in a pure state, and without blemish, 371
it is the discipline taught by the Sugata[2]
my teacher's instruction,
instruction that I revere,
why do you keep me from my way?

Your mind is disturbed, mine is not, 372
you are impure, I am not,
my mind is free wherever I am.
Why do you keep me from my way?

373 daharā ca apāpikā casi kiṃ te pabbajjā karissati
nikkhipa kāsāyacīvaraṃ ehi ramāmase pupphite vane.

374 madhurañ ca pavanti sabbaso kusumarajena samuṭṭhitā dumā
paṭhamavasanto sukho utu ehi ramāmase pupphite vane.

375 kusumitasikharā va[1] pādapā abhigajjanti va māluteritā
kā tuyhaṃ rati bhavissati yadi ekā vanam otarissasi.[2]

376 vāḷamigasaṅghasevitaṃ kuñjaramattakareṇuloḷitaṃ
asahāyikā gantum icchasi rahitaṃ bhiṃsanakaṃ mahāvanaṃ.

The rake

You are young and innocent, 373
how can going forth be right for you?
Come on, get rid of that yellow robe,
let's enjoy each other in this forest,
its flowers all in bloom.

The air is sweet, 374
the trees are erect, their pollen is everywhere,
come on, the beginning of spring is the season for
happiness,
let's enjoy each other in this forest,
its flowers all in bloom.

The trees are covered in flowers 375
like body-hairs standing on end,
they seem to moan in pleasure when the breeze blows,
what delights of love will there be for you
if you go into the forest all by yourself?

You want to go into the vast forest without a girlfriend, 376
it is frightening and lonely,
filled with herds of wild beasts,
it echoes with the choruses of female elephants excited by
a male.

377 tapanīyakatā va dhītikā vicarasi cittarathe va accharā
kāsikasukhumehi vaggubhi sobhasi suvasanehi nūpame.

378 ahaṃ tava vasānugo siyaṃ yadi viharemase kānanantare
na hi catthi[3] tayā piyattaro pāṇo kinnarimandalocane.

379 yadi me vacanaṃ karissasi sukhitā ehi agāram āvasa
pāsādanivātavāsinī parikammaṃ te karontu nāriyo.

380 kāsikasukhumāni dhāraya abhiropehi ca mālavaṇṇakaṃ
kañcanamaṇimuttakaṃ bahuṃ vividhaṃ ābharaṇaṃ
karomi te.

381 sudhotarajapacchadaṃ subhaṃ goṇakatūlikasanthataṃ
navaṃ
abhiruha sayanaṃ mahārahaṃ
candanamaṇḍitasāragandhikaṃ.

You will stand out, wandering about in the forest, 377
like a doll of gleaming gold[3]
or like a beautiful nymph in Chittaratha.[4]
What should I call you, when nothing compares to you,
you are exquisite, so lovely in those good clothes
and with your fine Kasi shawl.[5]

I would be at your command 378
if we were to live together in the forest,
no one is more dear to me than you,
lady with the bashful eyes of a *kinnari*.[6]

If you will do what I suggest, you will be happy. 379
Come, make a home with me,
you will live in the safety of a palace,
let women wait on you.

Wrap yourself in these Kasi shawls, 380
put on some make-up and perfume,
while I get all sorts of adornments,
gold, gems, and pearls, for you.

Climb into this new bed, it's so luxurious, 381
it's sweet-smelling from sandalwood,
beautiful, it has spreads, throws, and covers,
and above it is a pure-white canopy.

382 uppalaṃ va udakato uggataṃ[4] yathā taṃ
amanussasevitaṃ
evaṃ tuvaṃ brahmacārinī sakesu aṅgesu jaraṃ gamissasi.

383 kiṃ te idha sārasammataṃ kuṇapapūramhi
susānavaḍḍhane
bhedanadhamme kaḷevare yaṃ disvā vimano udikkhasi.

384 akkhīni ca turiyāriva kinnariyāriva pabbatantare
tava me nayanānudikkhiya[5] bhiyyo kāmaratī pavaḍḍhati.

385 uppalasikharopamāni te[6] vimale hāṭakasannibhe mukhe
tava me nayanāni dakkhiya bhiyyo kāmaguṇo pavaḍḍhati.

386 api dūragatā saramhase āyatapamhe visuddhadassane
na hi catthi[7] tayā piyatarā nayanā kinnarimandalocane.

Or, holy one, would you rather go to old age 382
with your body untouched,
like a blue lotus that rises from the water
but is untouched by human hands?

Subha

You really are out of your mind. 383
What is it that you see
when you look at this body,
filled as it is with things that have already died,[7]
destined as it is to fall apart only to fill a cemetery?

The rake

I see your eyes! They are like the eyes of a fawn,[8] 384
they are like the eyes of a *kinnari* in a mountain cave.
Seeing your eyes only increases my delight
in getting ready to make love to you.

Those eyes! Seeing them 385
like blue lotus buds on your golden face
only increases my desire
in getting ready to make love to you.

Even after you have gone far away, 386
I will remember you and your eyes,
your long eyelashes, your pure gaze,
lady with the bashful eyes of a *kinnari*,
there is nothing better than your eyes.

387 apathena payātum icchasi candaṃ kīḷanakaṃ gavesasi
merum laṅghetum icchasi yo tvaṃ buddhasutaṃ
maggayasi.

388 natthi hi loke sadevake rāgo yattha pi dāni me siyā
na pi naṃ jānāmi kīriso atha maggena hato samūlako.

389 iṅgālakuyā va ujjhito visapattoriva aggato kato
na pi naṃ passāmi kīriso atha maggena hato samūlako.

390 yassā siyā apaccavekkhitaṃ satthā vā anupāsito siyā
tvaṃ tādisikaṃ palobhaya jānantiṃ so imaṃ vihaññasi.

Subha

You lust after a daughter of the Buddha. 387
You must want to go where no one else has gone,
want the moon as a toy,
and want to jump over Mt. Meru[9] too.

In this world with its gods 388
there is nothing that I desire;
if something I would desire does exist,
I do not know what it is,
whatever it may be, the path of my teacher
has destroyed the urge for it down to the root.

I do not see that there could be anything worth desiring, 389
the path has destroyed the urge for things down to the
root;
if something does exist that I might feel an urge for,
the urge for it is like an ember that jumps from a fire pit
only to go out,
like a bowl of poison that evaporates untouched.

There may be people who have not thought things 390
through,
maybe there are others who have not seen the teacher,
you should lust after one of them,
but try to seduce someone who knows and you will suffer.

391 mayhaṃ hi akkuṭṭhavandite sukhadukkhe ca satī
upaṭṭhitā
saṅkhatam asubhan ti jāniya sabbattheva mano na limpati.

392 sāhaṃ sugatassa sāvikā maggaṭṭhaṅgikayānayāyinī
uddhaṭasallā anāsavā suññāgāragatā ramāmahaṃ.

393 diṭṭhā hi mayā sucittitā sombhā dārukapillakāni vā
tantīhi ca khīlakehi ca vinibaddhā vividhaṃ panaccakā.[8]

394 tamhuddhaṭe tantikhīlake vissaṭṭhe vikale paripakkhite[9]
avinde khaṇḍaso kate kimhi tattha manaṃ nivesaye.

395 tathūpamā[10] dehakāni maṃ tehi dhammehi vinā na
vattanti
dhammehi vinā na vattati kimhi tattha manaṃ nivesaye.

396 yathā haritālena makkhitaṃ addasa cittikaṃ bhittiyā
kataṃ
tamhi te viparītadassanaṃ saññā[11] mānusikā niratthikā.

My mindfulness stands firm 391
in the middle of scolding and praising,
happiness and suffering,
knowing that what is constructed[10] is foul,
my mind does not get stuck anywhere.

I am a disciple of the Sugata,[11] 392
traveling in the vehicle that can only go on the eightfold
path.
The dart is pulled out,[12]
the depravities that ooze out from within are wasted away,
I am happy that I have gone to a deserted place.

I have seen painted dolls and puppets dancing about, 393
held up and held together by sticks and string.

When the sticks and strings are cut, 394
let go of, thrown away, and scattered,
broken into bits that can't be seen—
what would you fix your mind on there?

My body parts are like that,[13] 395
they don't exist without smaller bits,
and the body itself doesn't exist without those parts—
what would you fix your mind on there?

You saw some figures painted on a wall, 396
colored with yellow that makes their bodies seem lifelike,[14]
but what you saw is the opposite of what you think,
you thought you saw humans when none are there.

397 māyaṃ viya aggato kataṃ supinanteva suvaṇṇapādapaṃ
upagacchasi andha rittakaṃ janamajjheriva
rupparūpakaṃ.

398 vaṭṭaniriva koṭarohitā majjhe bubbuḷakā saassukā
pīḷakoḷikā cettha jāyati vividhā cakkhuvidhā ca[12] piṇḍitā.

399 uppāṭiya cārudassanā na ca pajjittha[13] asaṅgamānasā
handa te cakkhuṃ harassu taṃ tassa narassa adāsi tāvade.

400 tassa ca viramāsi tāvade rāgo tattha khamāpayī ca naṃ
sotthi siyā brahmacārinī na puno edisakaṃ bhavissati.

401 āsādiya edisaṃ janaṃ aggiṃ pajjalitaṃ va liṅgiya
gaṇhissaṃ[14] āsīvisaṃ viya api nu sotthi siyā khamehi no.

402 muttā ca tato sā bhikkhunī agamī buddhavarassa santikaṃ
passiya varapuññalakkhaṇaṃ cakkhu āsi yathāpurāṇakan
ti.

Blind one, you run after things that are not there, 397
things that are like a magician's illusion
or a tree of gold seen in a dream.

Eyes are just little balls in various shapes. 398
With its tears, an eye is a bubble of water between the
eyelids,
like a little ball of lac in the hollow of a tree,[15]
and milky mucus comes out of it.

Spoken by those who compiled the Scriptures

Then[16] the one who was so pleasing to look at, 399
her mind unattached and with no regard for her eye,
gouged it out and gave it to that man, saying,
"Here, take the eye, it's yours."

His sexual passion ended right there forever 400
and he begged her forgiveness, saying,
"Holy one, be whole again, this won't happen again.

"Wronging a person is like embracing fire, 401
it's as if I handled a poisonous snake,
be whole again, forgive me."

That nun who was freed[17] went to where the Buddha was, 402
and when she saw the beautiful signs of his excellence on
his body,[18]
her eye became as it was before.

cattālīsanipāto

isidāsī

403 nagaramhi kusumanāme pāṭaliputtamhi pathaviyā maṇḍe
sakyakulakulīnāyo dve bhikkhuniyo hi guṇavatiyo.

404 isidāsī tattha ekā dutiyā bodhī therī sīlasampannā ca
jhānajjhāyanaratā yo bahussutā yo dhutakilesāyo.

405 tā piṇḍāya caritvā bhattattham̧ kariya dhotapattāyo
rahitamhi sukhanisinnā imā girā abbhudīresum̧.

406 pāsādikāsi ayye isidāsi vayo pi te aparihīno
kim̧ disvāna vyālikam̧ athāsi nekkhammam anuyuttā.

407 evam̧ anuyuñjiyamānā sārahite dhammadesanākusalā
isidāsī vacanam abravi suṇa bodhi yathamhi pabbajitā.

A POEM WITH ABOUT FORTY VERSES

Isidasi

Spoken by those who compiled the Scriptures

In[1] Pataliputta, the city named after a flower[2] 403
and which is in the finest part of the earth,
there were two nuns, each with excellent qualities,
each from good families in the Sakya clan.

Isidasi was one and the nun Bodhi was the other, 404
each virtuous and learned,
they delighted in meditation and study,
all defiling compulsions destroyed.

After they ate their alms and washed their bowls, 405
while sitting happily in a secluded place,
they sang out these important words.

Spoken by Bodhi

You are so lovely, lady Isidasi, none of your youth is lost, 406
what did you see that was so wrong
that it made you intent on renunciation?

Spoken by those who compiled the Scriptures

When in that secluded place she was called to account, 407
Isidasi, who was skilled as a preacher, said,
"Listen, Bodhi, to how I went forth."

408 ujjeniyā puravare mayhaṃ pitā sīlasaṃvuto seṭṭhi
tassamhi ekadhītā piyā manāpā ca dayitā ca.

409 atha me sāketato varakā āgacchum uttamakulīnā
seṭṭhī pahūtaratano tassa mamaṃ suṇham adāsi tāto.

410 sassuyā sasurassa ca sāyaṃ pātaṃ paṇāmam upagamma
sirasā karomi pāde vandāmi yathamhi anusiṭṭhā.

411 yā mayhaṃ sāmikassa bhaginiyo bhātuno parijano
tam ekavarakam pi disvā ubbiggā āsanaṃ dadāmi.

412 annena ca pānena ca khajjena ca yañ ca tattha sannihitaṃ
chādemi upanayāmi ca demi ca yaṃ yassa patirūpaṃ.

413 kālena upaṭṭhahitvā gharaṃ samupagamāmi ummāre
dhovantī hatthapāde pañjalikā sāmikaṃ upemi ca.

Isidasi

My father was an eminent man of wealth in Ujjeni, 408
he was virtuous too.
I was his only daughter, dear to him,
a pleasure to him, the focus of his kindness.

Then suitors came from Saketa to ask for me, 409
all from a noble family,
among them was another eminent man of great wealth.
Father gave me as a daughter-in-law to him.

I waited on my mother-in-law and my father-in-law, 410
morning and night, I placed my head on their feet,
I honored them just as I had been taught.

I would get flustered if I saw 411
the sisters of my husband,
his brothers, or his servants,
even if I saw my husband himself,
and I would give up my seat.

I tried to please them with all sorts of foods and drinks, 412
I brought in whatever delicacy was available
and gave each whatever was preferred.

Up and about at an early hour, 413
I would come to the house and pause at the door,
after washing my hands and feet
I would come to my husband with my hands folded.

414 kocchaṃ pasādaṃ añjaniñ ca ādāsakañ ca gaṇhitvā
parikammakārikā viya sayam eva patiṃ vibhūsemi.

415 sayam eva odanaṃ sādhayāmi sayam eva bhājanaṃ
dhovantī
mātā va ekaputtakaṃ tathā bhattāraṃ paricarāmi.

416 evaṃ maṃ bhattikataṃ anurattaṃ kārikaṃ nihatamānaṃ
uṭṭhāyikaṃ analasaṃ sīlavatiṃ dussate bhattā.

417 so mātarañ ca pitarañ ca bhaṇati āpucchahaṃ gamissāmi
isidāsiyā na vacchaṃ ekāgārehaṃ saha vatthuṃ.

418 mā evaṃ putta avaca isidāsī paṇḍitā parivyattā
uṭṭhāyikā analasā kiṃ tuyhaṃ na rocate putta.

419 na ca me hiṃsati kiñci na cāhaṃ isidāsiyā saha vacchaṃ
dessāva me alaṃ me apucchāhaṃ gamissāmi.

420 tassa vacanaṃ suṇitvā sassūsasuro ca maṃ apucchiṃsu
kissa tayā aparaddhaṃ bhaṇa vissatthā yathābhūtaṃ.

I brought a comb and an ornament, 414
a box of eye ointment, and a mirror,
and I groomed my own husband well,
as a servant would.

I cooked rice in milk for him, then washed his bowl myself, 415
I looked after my husband, like a mother would for her
only son.

My husband only did me wrong, 416
while I was virtuous, not lazy, and submissive,
he only humiliated me when I waited on him lovingly.

He would say to his mother and father, 417
"I want to leave, I don't need your permission to go,
I will not live with Isidasi,
I don't want to live in the same house as her."

"Don't speak like that, son, 418
Isidasi is wise and beautiful,
she gets up early and is not lazy.
What don't you like, son?"

"It's not that she hurts me, it's just that I can't stand her, 419
I hate her and I have had enough,
I want to leave, I don't need your permission to go."

After they heard that, my parents-in-law asked me, 420
"What have you been up to?
Open up, tell what really happened."

421 na pihaṃ aparajjhaṃ kiñci na pi hiṃsemi na bhaṇāmi
dubbacanaṃ kiṃ sakkā kātuyye yaṃ maṃ viddessate
bhattā.

422 te maṃ pitugharaṃ patinayiṃsu vimanā dukkhena
avibhūtā puttaṃ anurakkhamānā jitamhase rūpiniṃ
lakkhiṃ.

423 atha maṃ adāsi tāto aḍḍhassa gharamhi dutiyakulikassa
tato upaḍḍhasuṅkena yena maṃ vindatha seṭṭhi.

424 tassa pi gharamhi māsaṃ avasi atha so pi maṃ paṭicchasi
dāsī va upaṭṭhahantiṃ adūsikaṃ sīlasampannaṃ.

425 bhikkhāya ca vicarantaṃ damakaṃ dantaṃ me pitā
bhaṇati
so hi si me jāmātā nikkhipa pontiñ ca ghaṭikañ ca.

426 so pi vasitvā pakkhaṃ atha tā taṃ bhaṇati dehi me
pontiṃ ghaṭikañ ca mallakañ ca puna pi bhikkhaṃ
carissāmi.

427 atha naṃ bhaṇatī tāto ammā sabbo ca me ñātigaṇavaggo
kiṃ te na kīrati idha bhaṇa khippaṃ taṃ te karihi ti.

"I didn't do anything wrong, I never hurt him, 421
I never even said an untoward word,
what should I do when my husband hates me so much?"

They took me back to my father's house unhappily, 422
not understanding what had happened, they said,
"While watching over our son, we lost Lakshmi[3]
incarnate."

Then Father gave me to a rich man from a second family. 423
That eminent man of wealth got me but with only half the
dowry.

I lived in his house for just a month, 424
virtuous, innocent, attending to his wants,
but he treated me more like a slave than a wife.

My father then spoke to an ascetic wandering for alms, 425
a man who had tamed himself and could tame others.
"Be my daughter's husband in my house,
throw away the rags you are wearing and your bowl."

He lived with us for two weeks before he said to Father, 426
"Give me back the rags and the bowl, I will wander for
alms again."

Father said to him, and then my mother and all my 427
relatives,
"What hasn't been done for you? Just say it and she will do
it."

428 evaṃ bhaṇito bhaṇati yadi me attā sakkoti alaṃ mayhaṃ
isidāsiyā na sahavacchaṃ ekaghareham saha vatthuṃ.

429 vissajjito gato so aham pi ekā kinī vicintemi
apucchitūna gacchaṃ maritāye vā pabbajissaṃ vā.

430 atha ayyā jinadattā āgacchī gocarāya caramānā
tātakulaṃ vinayadharī bahussutā sīlasampannā.

431 taṃ disvā na amhākaṃ uṭṭhāyāsanaṃ tassā paññāpayiṃ
nisinnāya ca pāde vanditvā bhojanaṃ adāsiṃ.

432 annena ca pānena ca khajjena ca yañ ca tattha sannihitaṃ
santappayitvā avacaṃ ayye icchāmi pabbajitun ti.

433 atha maṃ bhaṇati tāto idheva puttaka carāhi tvaṃ
dhammaṃ
annena ca pānena ca tappaya samaṇe dvijātī ca.

434 athāhaṃ bhaṇāmi tātaṃ rodantī añjaliṃ paṇāmetvā
pāpaṃ hi mayā pakataṃ kammaṃ taṃ nijjaressāmi.

He replied, "Whatever I can do for myself is enough for me, 428
I don't want to live in the same house as Isidasi."

No one stopped him when he went off and I was left alone, 429
I thought, "Either I will sneak off to die or I will go forth."

Then Jinadatta, wandering for food, came to Father's house. 430
It was obvious that she was disciplined, learned, and virtuous.

As soon as I saw her, I got up from my seat and gave it to her; 431
when she had sat, I bowed to her feet and gave her food.

I tried to please her with all sorts of foods and drinks, 432
I brought in whatever delicacy was available,
And then I said, "Madam, I wish to go forth."

Father immediately said to me, "Child, you can practice 433
the Buddha's teaching here at home, be satisfied
with giving food and drink to ascetics and the twice-born."

I started to cry and showing my respect with my hands joined together, 434
I said to Father, "I have done evil
and I must destroy that karma."

435 atha maṃ bhaṇati tāto pāpuṇa bodhiñ ca aggadhammañ ca
nibbānañ ca labhassu yaṃ sacchikari dvipadaseṭṭho.

436 mātāpitū abhivādayitvā sabbañ ca ñātigaṇavaggaṃ
sattāhaṃ pabbajitā tisso vijjā aphassayiṃ.

437 jānāmi attano satta jātiyo yassayaṃ phalaṃ vipāko
taṃ tava ācikkhissaṃ taṃ ekamanā nisāmehi.

438 nagaramhi erakacche suvaṇṇakāro ahaṃ pahutadhano
yobbanamadena matto so paradāraṃ asevihaṃ.

439 sohaṃ tato cavitvā nirayamhi apaccisaṃ ciraṃ
pakko tato ca uṭṭhahitvā makkaṭiyā kucchimhi okkamiṃ.

440 sattāhajātakaṃ maṃ mahākapi yūthapo nillacchesi
tassetaṃ kammaphalaṃ yathā pi gantvāna paradāraṃ.

441 sohaṃ tato cavitvā kālaṃ karitvā sindhavāraññe
kāṇāya ca khañjāya ca eḷakiyā kucchim okkamiṃ.

Father relented and said, "May you attain awakening, 435
the highest dhamma and freedom as well,
may you attain everything that the best of humans
experience."

I honored my parents and then all of my relatives, 436
I went forth and seven days later
I knew the three things that most don't know.[4]

I know my last seven births and what caused 437
all that has happened to me in this life,
I will tell that to you, listen carefully to it.

I was once a wealthy goldsmith in Erakaccha city, 438
but my youth made my head spin,
and I had sex with the wife of another.

When I died, I cooked in hell for a long time, 439
and then rising from there, I entered the womb of a
monkey.

A great monkey, the leader of the troop, 440
castrated me when I was seven days old,
this was the karmic fruit for the adultery.

It was in the Sindhava forest where I died, 441
and then I entered the womb of a one-eyed, lame goat.

442 dvādasavassāni ahaṃ nillacchito dārake parivahitvā
kiminā vaṭṭo akallo yathā pi gantvāna paradāraṃ.

443 sohaṃ tato cavitvā govāṇijakassa gāviyā jāto
vaccho lākhā tambo nillacchito dvādase māse.

444 voḍhūna naṅgalam ahaṃ sakaṭañ ca dhārayāmi
andho vaṭṭo akallo yathā pi gantvā na paradāraṃ.

445 sohaṃ tato cavitvā vīthiyā dāsiyā ghare jāto
neva mahilā na puriso yathā pi gantvā na paradāraṃ.

446 tiṃsativassamhi mato sākaṭikakulamhi dārikā jātā
kapaṇamhi appabhoge aṇikapurisapātabahulamhi.[1]

447 taṃ maṃ tato satthavāho ussannāya vipulāya vaḍḍhiyā
okaḍḍhati vilapantiṃ acchinditvā kulagharassa.

448 atha soḷasame vasse disvāna maṃ pattayobbanaṃ
kaññaṃ orundhatassa putto giridāso nāma nāmena.

As a goat, I was castrated, 442
and I was always afflicted by vermin,
children rode me for twelve years,
all for my adultery.

After my death as a goat, I was given birth by a cow 443
belonging to a cattle-trader, a calf with the red color of lac,
I was castrated when I was twelve months old.

I had to draw carts, plows, and wagons, 444
I was blind, always afflicted, and unhealthy, all for my adultery.

After my death as a bullock, I was born on the street, 445
in the household of a slave,
I was neither male or female,
I was the third sex, all for my adultery.

I died when I was thirty and was reborn a carter's daughter, 446
in a family that was miserable and poor, always
under attack from many creditors.

When the interest that was owed had accumulated and was large, 447
a caravan-leader took me from the house by force,
and dragged me away crying.

His son Giridasa noticed that I had reached puberty 448
in my sixteenth year and he claimed me as his own.

449 tassa pi aññā bhariyā sīlavatī guṇavatī yasavatī ca
anurattā bhattāraṃ tassāhaṃ viddesanam akāsiṃ.

450 tassetaṃ kammaphalaṃ yaṃ maṃ apakīritūna gacchanti
dāsī va upaṭṭhahantiṃ tassa pi anto kato mayā ti.

He already had another wife, 449
someone virtuous, of good qualities, with a good
reputation,
she loved her husband, but I made her hate me.

So it was all the fruit of my karma, 450
when they all threw me away and left,
even when I waited on them like a slave,
but now I have put an end to all that.

mahānipāto

sumedhā

451 mantāvatiyā nagare rañño koñcassa aggamahesiyā
dhītā āsiṃ sumedhā pasāditā sāsanakarehi.

452 sīlavatī cittakathā bahussutā buddhasāsane vinītā
mātāpitaro upagamma bhaṇati ubhayo nisāmetha.

453 nibbānābhiratāhaṃ asassataṃ bhavagataṃ yadi pi dibbaṃ
kim aṅgaṃ pana tucchā kāmā appassādā bahuvighātā.

454 kāmā kaṭukā āsīvisūpamā yesu mucchitā bālā
te dīgharattaṃ niraye samappitā haññante dukkhitā.

THE GREAT CHAPTER

Sumedha

When[1] I was Sumedha, 451
the daughter of King Konca of Mantavati and his chief queen,
I was converted[2] by those who live what the Buddha taught.

Through them, I became virtuous, eloquent, learned, 452
disciplined in the teaching of the Buddha,
and I came to my parents and said,
"May you both listen carefully.

"I delight in nibbana, 453
everything about life is uncertain
even if it is the life of a god,
why would I delight in things not worth desiring,
things with so little pleasure and so much annoyance.

"Everything that the senses desire is bitter, 454
but fools swoon over such poisonous things
only to end up in hell for a long time,
there they suffer and in the end they are destroyed.

455 socanti pāpakammā vinipāte pāpavuddhino
sadā kāyena ca vācāya ca manasā ca asaṃvutā.

456 bālā te duppaññā acetanā dukkhasamudayoruddhā
desante ajānantā na bujjhare ariyasaccāni.

457 saccāni amma buddhavaradesitāni te bahutarā ajānantā
ye abhinandanti bhavagataṃ pihenti devesu upapattiṃ.

458 devesu pi upapatti asassatā bhavagate aniccamhi
na ca santasanti bālā punappunaṃ jāyitabbassa.

459 cattāro vinipātā dve ca gatiyo kathañci labbhanti
na ca vinipātagatānaṃ pabbajjā atthi nirayesu.

“Such fools cannot control what they do 455
with their body, speech, or mind,
weeping wherever they are punished
for their own evil actions,
always increasing evil for themselves.

“They are fools, unwise, heedless, 456
locked up in their own suffering as it arises,
even when someone tries to teach them,
they are oblivious, not realizing
that they are living out the noble truths.[3]

“Mother, most people cannot understand 457
these truths taught by the Buddha,
they take pleasure in everything about life
and they long to be born among gods.

“Even birth among gods is uncertain, 458
it is only birth in another place just as impermanent,
but somehow fools are not terrified
of being born again and again.

“There are four places of punishment 459
and two other ones where we are somehow reborn.[4]
There is no going forth[5] from hell
once you are there to be punished.

460 anujānātha maṃ ubhayo pabbajituṃ dasabalassa pāvacane
appossukkā ghaṭissaṃ jātimaraṇappahānāya.

461 kiṃ bhavagate abhinanditena kāyakalinā asārena
bhavataṇhāya nirodhā anujānātha pabbajissāmi.

462 buddhānaṃ uppādo vivajjito akkhaṇo khaṇo laddho
sīlāni brahmacariyaṃ yāvajīvaṃ na dūseyyaṃ.

463 evaṃ bhaṇati sumedhā mātāpitaro na tāva āhāraṃ
āhariyāmi gahaṭṭhā maraṇavasaṃ gatā va hessāmi.

464 mātā dukkhitā rodati pitā ca assā sabbaso samabhihato
ghaṭenti saññāpetuṃ pāsādatale chamā patitaṃ.

465 uṭṭhehi puttaka kiṃ socitena dinnāsi vāraṇavatimhi
rājā aṇīkadatto[1] abhirūpo tassa tvaṃ dinnā.

"Give me permission, both of you, to go forth now 460
in the teaching of the Buddha, the one with ten powers,[6]
I do not have other responsibilities and I will exert myself
to make an end of birth and death.

"I am finished with delighting in just being alive, 461
I am finished too with the misfortune of having a body,
Give me permission and I will go forth
for the sake of ending the craving for existence.

"When Buddhas appear 462
bad luck can be avoided and good luck can be had;
for as long as I live, I will keep my moral precepts,
I will not defame the holy life."

Then Sumedha said to her mother and father, 463
"I will not eat any more food as a householder,
if I do not receive permission to go forth,[7]
I will be in your house, but I might as well be dead."

Her mother suffered and cried 464
and her father's face was covered with tears,
they tried to reason with Sumedha
who had fallen to the palace floor.

"Get up, child, what are these tears for? 465
You are already promised in marriage,
you have been given to handsome King Anikadatta
who is in Varanavati.

466 aggamahesī bhavissasi aṇīkadattassa rājino bhariyā
sīlāni brahmacariyaṃ pabbajjā dukkarā puttaka.

467 rajje āṇā dhanam issariyaṃ bhogā sukhā daharikāsi
bhuñjāhi kāmabhoge vāreyyaṃ hotu te putta.[2]

468 atha ne bhaṇati sumedhā mā īdisikāni bhavagataṃ asāraṃ
pabbajjā vā hohiti maraṇaṃ vā me na ceva vāreyyaṃ.

469 kimi va pūtikāyam asuciṃ savanagandhaṃ bhayānakaṃ
kuṇapaṃ abhisaṃviseyyaṃ bhastaṃ asakiṃ paggharaṇaṃ
asucipuṇṇaṃ.

470 kim iva tāhaṃ jānantī vikulakaṃ maṃsasoṇitupalittaṃ
kimikulālasakuṇabhattaṃ[3] kaḷebaraṃ kissa diyyatīti.

471 nibbuyhati susānaṃ aciraṃ kāyo apetaviññāṇo
chuddho kaḷiṅgaraṃ viya jigucchamānehi ñātīhi.

"You will be the wife of King Anikadatta, 466
his chief queen, and remember, child,
keeping moral precepts, living the holy life,
going forth, all that is hard to do.

"In kingship, there is authority, wealth, power, 467
things to enjoy and happiness.
You are a young girl, enjoy the pleasures of the body
and enjoy wealth. Let your wedding take place, child."

Sumedha answered them, 468
"It's not like that at all, existence is worthless,
I will either go forth or I will die,
but I won't get married.

"Why should I cling, like a worm, 469
to a body that will only turn into a corpse,
a sack always oozing, frightening, stinking
foul and putrid, filled with foul things?[8]

"I certainly know what the body is like. 470
It is repulsive, a corpse, food for birds and worms,
covered with flesh and blood,
so why is it to be given in marriage?

"This body will soon be carried, 471
without consciousness, to the cemetery,
it will be discarded like a log
by disgusted relatives.

472 chuddhūna taṃ susāne parabhattaṃ nhāyanti jigucchantā
niyakā mātāpitaro kiṃ pana sādhāraṇā janatā.

473 ajjhositā asāre kalevare aṭṭhinhārusaṅghāte
kheḷassuccārapassavaparipuṇṇe[4] pūtikāyamhi.

474 yo naṃ vinibbhujitvā abbhantaram assa bāhiraṃ kayirā
gandhassa asahamānā sakā pi mātā jiguccheyya.

475 khandhadhātuāyatanaṃ saṅkhataṃ jātimūlakaṃ
dukkhaṃ
yoniso anuvicinantī vāreyyaṃ kissa iccheyyaṃ.

476 divase divase tisatti satāni navanavā pateyyuṃ kāyamhi
vassasataṃ pi ca ghāto seyyo dukkhassa ceva khayo.

"After they have thrown it away as food for others, 472
even one's own mother and father, disgusted, wash
themselves,
and it has to be even more disgusting for everyone.

"People cling to this body, 473
even though it has no essence,
and is only a tangle of bones and sinews,
a foul body filled with spit, tears, feces, and urine.

"If one's own mother were to open it up 474
and pull what is inside of it outside,
even she would not be able to stand the stench
and would be disgusted by it.

"If I consider carefully what makes a person 475
the senses and their objects, the basic elements
that make up everything,[9] I see that all of it is constructed,

it is all rooted in birth and is the condition for suffering,
so why would I want to get married?

"Even if three hundred new swords were to cut my body 476
day after day for a hundred years,
it would be worth it
if it brought an end to suffering.

477 ajjhupagacche ghātaṃ yo viññāyevaṃ satthuno vacanaṃ
dīgho tesaṃ saṃsāro punappunaṃ haññamānānaṃ.

478 devesu manussesu ca tiracchānayoniyā asurakāye
petesu ca nirayesu ca aparimitā dissante ghātā.

479 ghātā nirayesu bahū vinipātagatassa pīḷiyamānassa
devesu pi attāṇaṃ nibbānasukhā paraṃ natthi.

480 pattā te nibbānaṃ ye yuttā dasabalassa pāvacane
appossukkā ghaṭenti jātimaraṇappahānāya.

481 ajjeva tātabhinikkhamissaṃ bhogehi kiṃ asārehi
nibbinnā me kāmā vantasamā tālavatthukatā.

"Anyone would put this carnage on themselves 477
once they understood the instruction of the teacher,
samsara is long for those
who are reborn again and again
only to be killed again and again.

"There is no end 478
to the carnage that occurs in samsara,
among gods and humans,
among animals, asuras, and hungry ghosts, and also in hells.[10]

"There is so much carnage 479
for those who are in hells for punishment,
but even for gods there is no safe place.
There is nothing better than the happiness of nibbana.

"Those who have reached nibbana 480
are the ones who are disciplined
by the teaching of the one with ten powers,[11]
living at ease, they strive to end birth and death.

"Today, Father, I will go renounce, 481
what good are insubstantial pleasures?
I am fed up with what pleases the senses,
all of it is like vomit,
like a palm-tree with its top cut off."[12]

482 sā cevaṃ bhaṇati pitaram aṇīkadatto ca yassa sā dinnā
upayāsi vāraṇavate vāreyyaṃ upaṭṭhite kāle.

483 atha asitanicitamuduke kese khaggena chindiya
sumedhā pāsādaṃ pidahitvā paṭhamajjhānaṃ samāpajji.

484 sā ca tahiṃ samāpannā anīkaratto ca āgato nagaraṃ
pāsāde ca sumedhā aniccasaññā subhāveti.

485 sā ca manasi karoti aṇīkadatto ca āruhī turitaṃ
maṇikanakabhūsitaṅgo katañjalī yācati sumedhaṃ.

486 rajje āṇā dhanam issariyaṃ bhogā sukhā daharikāsi
bhuñjāhi kāmabhoge kāmasukhā dullabhā loke.[5]

487 nissaṭṭhaṃ te rajjaṃ bhoge bhuñjassu dehi dānāni
mā dummanā ahosi mātā pitaro te dukkhitā.

While she was speaking in this way to her father, 482
Anikadatta, to whom she was promised in marriage,
arrived in the city of Varanavati[13] at the time set for the
wedding.

Right at that moment, Sumedha cut her hair, 483
black, thick, and soft, with a knife,
she went inside the palace and closed herself inside it
and closed herself inside herself into the first *jhāna*.[14]

Anikadatta had reached the city 484
at the same time that she went into that happy state,
inside the palace, Sumedha developed
her perceptions of impermanence.

While she was focusing her attention in meditation, 485
Anikadatta entered the palace in a hurry,
his body even more beautiful with jewels and gold,
and he entreated Sumedha respectfully.

"In kingship, there is authority, wealth, power, 486
things to enjoy and happiness.
You are a young girl,
enjoy the pleasures of the body,[15]
happiness for the body is rare in this world.

"The kingdom is bestowed[16] on you, 487
enjoy what is meant to be enjoyed, and be generous,
do not be sad yourself, you are making your parents
suffer."

488 taṃ taṃ bhaṇati sumedhā kāmehi anatthikā vigatamohā
mā kāme abhinandi kāmesvādīnavaṃ passa.

489 cātuddīpo rājā mandhātā āsi kāmabhoginaṃ aggo
atitto kālaṅkato na cassa paripūritā icchā.

490 sattaratanāni vasseyya vuṭṭhimā dasadisā samantena
na catthi titti kāmānaṃ atittā va maranti narā.

491 asisūṇūpamā kāmā kāmā sappasiropamā
ukkūpamā anudahanti aṭṭhikaṅkhalasannibhā.[6]

492 aniccā addhuvā kāmā bahudukkhā mahāvisā
ayoguḷo va santatto aghamūlā dukhapphalā.

493 rukkhaphalūpamā kāmā maṃsapesūpamā dukhā
supinopamā vañcaniyā kāmā yācitakūpamā.

But Sumedha knew that the urges of the senses lead 488
nowhere
and her delusions about the world were gone.
She began to speak, "You should not delight
in the pleasures of the senses, look at the dangers in them.

"Mandhata[17] was a king of the known world, 489
no one had more wealth or pleasure than him,
but even he died unsatisfied,
his wants unfulfilled.

"Even if it were to rain every kind of jewel, 490
enough to fill the ten directions,
still there would be no satisfying the desires of the senses.
Humans always die unsatisfied.

"The pleasures of the senses are like a slaughterhouse, 491
they are like a snake's head, they burn like a torch,
they give as much pleasure as a skeleton.

"The pleasures of the senses are impermanent 492
inconstant, they come with sufferings,
they are strong poisons, a hot iron ball down the throat,
they are the root of pain, and suffering is their fruit.

"The pleasures of the senses are like the fruits of a tree,[18] 493
like pieces of meat, pain is what they are,
the pleasures of the senses deceive like a dream,
they are like borrowed goods.

494 sattisūlūpamā kāmā rogo gaṇḍo aghaṃ nighaṃ
aṅgārakāsusadisā aghamūlaṃ bhayaṃ vadho.

495 evaṃ bahudukkhā kāmā akkhātā antarāyikā
gacchatha na me bhagavate vissāso atthi attano.

496 kiṃ mama paro karissati attano sīsamhi ḍayhamānamhi
anubandhe jarāmaraṇe tassa ghātāya ghaṭitabbaṃ.

497 dvāraṃ avāpuritvānahaṃ mātāpitaro aṇīkadattañ ca
disvāna chamaṃ nisinne rodante idam avocaṃ.

498 dīgho bālānaṃ saṃsāro punappunañ ca rodataṃ
anamatagge pitu maraṇe bhātu vadhe attano ca vadhe.

499 assu thaññaṃ rudhiraṃ saṃsāraṃ anamataggato saratha
sattānaṃ saṃsarataṃ sarāhi aṭṭhīnaṃ ca sannicayaṃ.

"The pleasures of the senses are like swords and stakes, 494
like disease, like an abscess, painful and hurtful,
they are like a pit of burning coals,
the root of pain, fearful and fatal.

"The pleasures of the senses bring many sufferings, 495
those who know call them hindrances,
you should go,
I myself don't trust existence.

"What can another do for me 496
when his own head is on fire?
When old age and death are right behind one,
one must try to end them."

At that point, Sumedha opened the door 497
and saw her mother and father, and also Anikadatta
all seated on the floor, crying,
and she said this to them:

"Samsara is long for fools 498
and for those who cry over and over
over the death of a father
or the killing of a brother or their own death.

"When you remember samsara 499
as it really is for beings,
remember the tears, the mothers' milk, the blood,
the mountain of bones of those born again and again.

500 sara caturodadhī upanīte assuthaññarudhiramhi
sara ekakappam aṭṭhīnaṃ sañcayaṃ vipulena samaṃ.

501 anamatagge saṃsarato mahiṃ jambudīpam upanītaṃ
kolaṭṭhimattaguḷikā mātāmātusveva nappahonti.

502 sara tiṇakaṭṭhasākhāpalāsaṃ upanītaṃ anamataggato
caturaṅgulikā ghaṭikā pitupitusveva nappahonti.

503 sara kāṇakacchapaṃ pubbasamudde aparato ca
yugacchiddaṃ
sara tassa ca paṭimukkaṃ manussalābhamhi opammaṃ.

504 sara rūpaṃ pheṇapiṇḍopamassa kāyakalino asārassa
khandhe passa anicce sarāhi niraye bahuvighāte.

505 sara kaṭasivaḍḍhente punappunaṃ tāsu tāsu jātīsu
sara kumbhīlabhayāni ca sarāhi cattāri saccāni.

"Think of the oceans when remembering the tears, 500
the mothers' milk, and the blood,
think of Mt. Vipula[19]
when counting the bones that just one being has had.

"If the whole continent of Jambudvipa 501
were broken up into little balls
the size of small fruits,
the number of them would still be less
than the number of mothers and grandmothers you have had.

"Think about all the grass, sticks, and leaves there are, 502
even if they were broken into smaller pieces
they would still be less than the fathers and grandfathers you have had.

"Remember the blind turtle in the eastern sea 503
and the hole in the yoke floating in another ocean,
remember how the turtle put his head through the yoke,
that is our chances of having a human birth.

"Remember the body, it has no essence inside, 504
a misfortune in itself, no more than a ball of foam,
look at what makes a person, it is all impermanent,
think of the hells filled with carnage.

"Remember all those who keep on filling cemeteries, 505
remember to fear becoming a 'crocodile,'[20]
remember the four noble truths.

506 amatamhi vijjamāne kiṃ tava pañcakaṭukena pītena
sabbāhi kāmaratiyo kaṭukatarā pañcakaṭukena.

507 amatamhi vijjamāne kiṃ tava kāmehi ye pariḷāhā
sabbāhi kāmaratiyo jalitā kuthitā kampitā santāpitā.

508 asapattamhi samāne kiṃ tava kāmehi ye bahū sapattā
rājaggicoraudakappiyehi sādhāraṇā kāmā bahū sapattā.

509 mokkhamhi vijjamāne kiṃ tava kāmehi yesu hi vadhabandho
kāmesu hi asakāmā vadhabandhadukkhāni anubhonti.

510 ādīpitā tiṇukkā gaṇhantaṃ dahanti neva muñcantaṃ
ukkopamā hi kāmā dahanti ye te na muñcanti.

"When you could taste sweet ambrosia,[21] 506
why would you want to taste the five bitter things?[22]
And the pleasures of the senses
are actually more bitter than the five bitter things.

"When the sweet ambrosia of the deathless exists, 507
why would you want the pleasures of the senses that are
painful?
All the delights of the senses burn, are rotten,
troubled, and are seething.

"When friends exist, 508
why would you want the pleasures of the senses
that are only so many enemies?
They are like kings, thieves, floods, and disliked people
in how harmful they are to you.

"When freedom exists, why would anyone want 509
imprisonment and execution?
In the pleasures of the senses, people experience
the sufferings of bondage and beatings against their will.

"A bundle of grass, when set on fire, 510
burns the one who holds it and does not let go,
the pleasures of the senses are like torches
that will not let go of anyone who held them.

511 mā appakassa hetu kāmasukhassa vipulaṃ jahī sukhaṃ
mā puthulomo va baḷisaṃ gilitvā pacchā vihaññasi.

512 kāmaṃ kāmesu damassu tāva sunakho va saṅkhalābaddho
kāhinti khu taṃ kāmā chātā sunakhaṃ va caṇḍālā.

513 aparimitañ ca dukkhaṃ bahūni ca cittadomanassāni
anubhohisi kāmesu yutto paṭinissaja addhuve kāme.

514 ajaramhi vijjamāne kiṃ tava kāmehi yesu jarā
maraṇavyādhigahitā sabbā sabbattha jātiyo.

515 idam ajaram idam amaraṃ idam ajarāmarapadam asokaṃ
asapattaṃ asambādhaṃ akhalitam abhayaṃ nirupatāpaṃ.

"Why abandon a big happiness 511
because of the little happiness that the urges of the senses
promise?
Do not suffer later like the *puthuloma* fish
who swallows the hook just to eat the bait.

"When among those things that please the senses, 512
control what the senses urge, just as a dog is held by a
chain,
otherwise the urges of the senses will kick you about
like a low-caste person does to a dog.

"If you get yoked to the pleasures of the senses, 513
you will experience no end of suffering,
so many sadnesses of the mind,
so give up such unreliable pleasures.

"When there can be no aging, 514
why would anyone want the pleasures of the senses,
since aging itself is in their midst,
just as sickness and death always come together with
birth?

"This is something that has no old age, it has no death, 515
this is the sorrowless state,
without old age and death,
without enmity, without crowding,
without failure, without fear, without trouble.

516 adhigatam idaṃ bahūhi amataṃ ajjā pi ca labhanīyam
idaṃ
yo yoniso payuñjati na ca sakkā aghaṭamānena.

517 evaṃ bhaṇati sumedhā saṅkhāragate ratim alabhamānā
anunentyaṇīkadattaṃ kese ca chamaṃ khipi sumedhā.

518 uṭṭhāya aṇīkadatto pañjaliko yāci tassā pitaraṃ so
vissajjetha sumedhaṃ pabbajituṃ vimokkhasaccadassaṃ.

519 Vissajjitā mātāpitūhi pabbaji sokabhayabhītā
cha abhiññā sacchikatā aggaphalaṃ sikkhamānāya.

520 acchariyaṃ abbhutaṃ taṃ nibbānaṃ āsi rājakaññāya
pubbenivāsacaritaṃ yathā vyākari pacchime kāle.

521 bhagavati koṇāgamane saṅghārāmamhi navanivesamhi
sakhiyo tisso janiyo vihāradānaṃ adāsimha.

"This state without death has been attained by many, 516
it should be attained today by us,
the one who applies himself easily can,
but it is not possible for one who does not strive."

As Sumedha spoke, she took no delight 517
in the constructed appearances of the world,[23]
but finally to convince Anikadatta,
she threw the hair she had cut off on the floor.

Anikadatta stood up and joined his hands respectfully, 518
he asked her father to allow Sumedha to go forth
so she could see nibbana and the four noble truths.

Allowed to go by her mother and father, 519
she went forth, frightened as she was by the sorrows that otherwise had to come,[24]
and she realized the six higher powers and the highest fruit[25]
while she was still being trained.

The attainment of nibbana for that king's daughter 520
was marvelous and unusual,
but equally so was what she said about her previous existences:

"When the Lord Buddha Konagamana[26] was 521
in a new residence in a monastery,
I was one of three woman friends
who gave a *vihara* to him

522 dasakkhattuṃ satakkhattuṃ dasasatakkhattuṃ satāni ca
satakkhattuṃ
devesu uppajjimha ko pana vādo manussesu.

523 devesu mahiddhikā ahumha mānusakamhi ko pana vādo
sattaratanassa mahesī itthiratanaṃ ahaṃ āsiṃ.

524 so hetu so pabhavo taṃ mūlaṃ sā va sāsane khantī
taṃ paṭhaṃ asamodhānaṃ taṃ dhammaratāya nibbānaṃ.

525 evaṃ karonti ye saddahanti vacanaṃ anomapaññassa
nibbindanti bhavagate nibbinditvā virajjantī ti.

"As a result of that, we were born among gods 522
ten times, one hundred times,
one thousand times, ten thousand times,
who can say how many times
we were born among humans just from that gift.

"When we were born among gods, we had great powers, 523
and it was the same when we were born among humans,
I was even the chief queen, the gem of a woman,
for a king who was a lord of the whole world.

"That gift was the root cause for my sense of peace 524
in the teaching of the Buddha,
that first encounter with that previous Buddha
led to nibbana for me who delighted in his dhamma.

"Those who trust the teaching 525
of the one who has perfect wisdom
and do what he teaches,
they become disgusted with existence,
and turning away from it,
they set themselves free."

ABBREVIATIONS

C Chatthasangiti edition of *Therīgāthā*. 1955 (1993).
H Hewavitarne edition of *Paramattha Dīpanī or the Commentary of the Therigatha*. Bihalpola Siri Dewarakkhita Thera, ed. 1918.
P Pali Text Society edition of *Therīgāthā*. Pischel 1883 (1966).
S Pali Text Society edition edition of *Saṃyutta-nikāya*. Vol. I. Feer 1884.

NOTES TO THE TEXT

ekakanipāto

1 P has another verse here, attributed to another Dhīrā:
dhīrā dhīrehi dhammehi bhikkhunī bhāvitindriyā
dhīrehi antimaṃ dehaṃ jetvā māram savāhanaṃ.

2 vimuccatī] ti vuccatī P, C.

3 Compare v. 13 with vv. 119, 176.

4 Compare the similar verse at S I.15.

dukanipāto

1 v. 19 = v. 82.

2 jentā] jentī P.

3 v. 21 = v. 45.

4 avasavattini] avasavattinī C. v. 37= vv. 42, 169. Compare with v. 40.

tikanipāto

1 avasavattini] avasavattinī C. Compare v.40 with 37, 42, 169.

2 v. 42 = vv. 37, 169. Compare with v. 40.

3 v. 43 = v. 69.

4 v. 45 = v. 21.

5 Compare v. 56 with v. 65.

6 v. 57 = S I.128.

7 v. 58 = vv. 141, 234. Compare v. 58 with S I.128.

8 v. 59 = vv. 62, 142, 188, 195, 203, 235.

9 vv. 60–61 = S I.129.

10 v. 62 = vv. 59, 142, 188, 195, 203, 235.

catukkanipāto

1 Compare v. 56 with v. 65.

pañcakanipāto

1 v. 69 = v. 43.

2 Compare v. 71 with vv. 227–228.

3 v. 82 = v. 19.

4 Compare v. 112 with vv. 117, 175.

5 v. 117 = v. 175.
6 vihariyāma] vihissāma P.
7 Compare vv. 119–121 with vv. 178–181.

chakkanipāto

1 Compare v. 140 with S I.131.
2 v. 141 = vv. 58, 234.
3 v. 142 = vv. 59, 62, 188, 195, 203, 235.
4 sampaṭivijjhahaṃ] P, C; apaṭivijjhahaṃ H.
5 meghassa] majjhassa P, C.
6 āriyaṭṭhaṅgiko] bhāvito aṭṭhaṅgiko C.
7 avasavattinī] avasavattini P. v. 169 = v. 37

sattakanipāto

1 v. 175 = v. 117.
2 viharāmi] vihissāmi P.
3 Compare vv. 178–181 with vv. 119–121.
4 v. 187 = v. 194.
5 v. 188 = vv. 59, 62, 142, 195, 203, 235.
6 v. 194 = v. 187.
7 v. 195 = vv. 59, 62, 142, 188, 203, 235.

aṭṭhakanipāto

1 v. 197] P, C; H omits.
2 v. 202 = vv. 187, 194.
3 v. 203 = vv. 59, 62, 142, 188, 195, 235.

ekādasanipāto

1 adhigacchi] adhigacchiṃ P, C.
2 apekkhihaṃ] avekkhiṃhaṃ C.

dvādasakanipāto

1 Compare vv. 227–228 with v. 71.
2 vv. 227–228] P, C; H omits.
3 v. 234 = vv. 58, 141.
4 v. 235 = vv. 59, 62, 142, 188, 195, 203.

soḷasanipāto

1 nakkā] nāgā P, C.

2 Compare v. 247 with vv. 249, 288.
3 vv. 249–251 = vv. 288*cd*–291.
4 vv. 249–251 = vv. 288*cd*–291.

vīsatinipāto

1 uttamaṅgajo] uttamaṅgabhu P.
2 jarāya sasalomagandhikaṃ] jarāya salomagandhikaṃ P; jarāyatha salomagandhikaṃ C.
3 kaṇha-] saṇha- P.
4 ca pitakā] yava pītakā P; cāsitā C.
5 nikūjihaṃ] nikūjitaṃ P.
6 yathā pāṭalippalitā] yathā pāṭalī dubbalikā P; yatha pāṭalibbalitā C.
7 thevikīva] te rindī va P.
8 Verse division for vv. 287–289 in P:
tuvaṃ hetaṃ pajānāsi puññakkhettaṃ anuttaraṃ
amham pi ca te samaṇā paṭigaṇhanti dakkhiṇaṃ.
patiṭṭhito hettha yañño vipulo no bhavissati.

sace bhāyasi dukkhassa sace te dukkhamappiyaṃ
upehi saraṇaṃ buddhaṃ dhammaṃ saṅghañca tādinaṃ
samādiyāhi sīlāni taṃ te atthāya hehiti.

9 vv. 288*cd*–291 = vv. 249–251.
10 sataputtāni] satta puttāni P.
11 samarocayi] P, C; samarocayiṃ H.
12 Verse divisions 325–339] P, C; H:
ehi sārathi gacchāhi rathaṃ nīyādayāhi maṃ
ārogyaṃ brāhmaṇiṃ vajja pabbajito dāni brāhmaṇo.

sujāto tīhi rattīhi tisso vijjā aphassayi
tato ca ratham ādāya sahassaṃ cāpi sārathi.

ārogyaṃ brāhmaṇiṃ voca pabbajito dāni brāhmaṇo
sujāto tīhi rattīhi tisso vijjā aphassayi.

etaṃ cahaṃ assarathaṃ sahassaṃ cāpi sārathi
tevijjaṃ brāhmaṇaṃ sutvā puṇṇapattaṃ dadāmi te.

tumheva hotu assaratho sahassañcā pi brāhmaṇi
aham pi pabbajissāmi varapaññassa santike.

hatthī gavassaṃ maṇikuṇḍalañca phītaṃ cimaṃ gahavibhavaṃ
pahāya
pitā pabbajito tuyhaṃ bhuñja bhogāni sundari tuvaṃ dāyādikā
kule.

hatthī gavassaṃ maṇikuṇḍalañca rammaṃ cimaṃ gahavibhavaṃ
pahāya
pitā pabbajito mayhaṃ puttasokena aṭṭito aham pi pabbajissāmi
bhātu
sokena aṭṭitā.

so te ijjhatu saṅkappo yaṃ tvaṃ patthesi sundari
uttiṭṭhapiṇḍo uñcho ca paṃsukūlaṃ ca cīvaraṃ.

etāni abhisambhontī paraloke anāsavā
sikkhamānāya me ayye dibbacakkhu visodhitaṃ.

pubbenivāsaṃ jānāmi yattha me vusitaṃ pure
tuvaṃ nissāya kalyāṇī therī saṅghassa sobhane.

tisso vijjā anuppattā kataṃ buddhassa sāsanaṃ
anujānāhi me ayye icche sāvatthi gantave.

sīhanādaṃ nadissāmi buddhaseṭṭhassa santike
passa sundari satthāraṃ hemavaṇṇaṃ harittacaṃ.

adantānaṃ dametāraṃ sambuddhamakutobhayaṃ
passa sundarim āyantiṃ vippamuttaṃ nirūpadhiṃ.

vītarāgaṃ visaṃyuttaṃ katakiccam anāsavaṃ.
bārāṇasīto nikkhamma tava santikam āgatā.

sāvikā te mahāvīra pāde vandati sundarī.
tuvaṃ buddho tuvaṃ satthā tuyhaṃ dhītamhi brāhmaṇa.

orasā mukhato jātā katakiccā anāsavā
tassā te svāgataṃ bhadde tato te adurāgataṃ.

evaṃ hi dantā āyanti satthu pādāni vandikā
vītarāgā visaṃyuttā katakiccā anāsavā ti.

13 therī saṅghassa] therīsaṅghassa P.
14 chaḍḍetvā] ṭhapetvā P.
15 P makes 2 verses of 342–344:
hitvānahaṃ ñātigaṇaṃ dāsakammakarāni ca
gāmakhettāni phītāni ramaṇīye pamodite
pahāyahaṃ pabbajitā sāpateyyam anappakaṃ.

evaṃ saddhāya nikkhamma saddhamme suppavedite
na me taṃ assa patirūpaṃ ākiñcaññaṃ hi patthaye
yā jātarūpaṃ rajataṃ ṭhapetvā punar āgame.

16 aggikkhandhasamā] aggikkhandhupamā P, C.
17 esa bhayo] eso sabhaya P.
18 lopo] ceso P, C.
19 caraṇabandhanā] maraṇabandhanā P, C.
20 ciitappamāthino] cittappamaddino C.
21 khipaṃ] khippaṃ P, C.
22 -visosakā] -visosanā P, C.
23 vihassāmi] vihissāmi P.

tiṃsanipāto

1 va] ca P, C.
2 otarissasi] ogāhissasi P; ogahissasi C.
3 catthi] matthi P.
4 uggataṃ] ubbhataṃ P; samuggataṃ C.
5 nayanānudikkhiya] nayanāni dakkhiya P, C.
6 uppalasikkharopamāni te] uppalasikkharopamānite P.
7 catthi] matthi P, C.
8 panaccakā] panaccitā P.
9 paripakkhite] paripakkate P.
10 tathūpamā] tathūpamaṃ P.
11 saññā] paññā P.
12 ca] va P.
13 pajjittha] <sajjittha> See Norman 2007: 175.
14 gaṇhissaṃ] gaṇhiya C.

cattālīsanipāto

1 aṇika-]dhanika- P, C.

mahānipāto

1 aṇīkadatto] anīkaratto P, C; mutatis mutandis throughout.
2 Compare v. 467 with v. 486.
3 kimikulālasakuṇabhattaṃ] C *v.l.*; kulālayaṃ sakuṇabhattaṃ P, H, C. See Norman 2007: 197.
4 kheḷassuccārapassavaparipuṇṇe] see Norman 2007: 199; kheḷassuccārassava paripuṇṇe H, C; kheḷassumucchāssavaparipuṇṇe P.
5 Compare v. 486 with v. 467.
6 aṭṭhikaṅkhalasannibhā] aṭṭhikaṅkalasannibhā C, aṭṭhikaṅkālasannibhā P.

NOTES TO THE TRANSLATION

Poems with One Verse

1 Therika was born in a rich Kshatriya family. She was given the name "Therika" because of her firm (*theri*), peaceful body. She had already been married when the Buddha came to where she lived. She was drawn to the way of life that he taught just by seeing him. Later she was taught by Mahapajapati Gotami, the stepmother of the Buddha and prominent among the nuns of the *Therīgāthā*, and she wanted to become a renunciant. Therika's husband did not permit her to go forth, but she practiced what she had been taught as a laywoman until her husband could see the transformations in her. He brought her to Mahapajapati Gotami for ordination. After Therika was ordained, Mahapajapati Gotami brought her to the Buddha. After he taught her, he said this verse to her. When she heard the verse, Therika was enlightened. Therika repeated what the Buddha said, making the verse an expression of her own experience.

The rubric in the canonical *Therīgāthā* (as in P and C) introduces the subject of this verse merely as "a certain unknown nun," Dhammapala takes the "therike" in the verse as her proper name [therīkā]; Norman takes it as descriptive diminutive and translates "little therī" (Norman 2007: 60).

2 Mutta was born in a wealthy Brahman family. She was ordained by Mahapajapati Gotami at the age of twenty and was very devoted to meditation. One day while Mutta was meditating, the Buddha sent a vision of himself to her and used it to speak this verse to her. When she was enlightened, she repeated the verse as her own. She repeated it again at the time of her death.

3 The demon that causes eclipses.

4 Punna was born in a wealthy family and was ordained by Mahapajapati Gotami. The Buddha sent a vision of himself to her and used it to speak this verse to her. The verse encouraged her to do what was necessary to become enlightened. She repeated the verse when she was enlightened to announce the achievement.

5 Tissa was born in the Sakya royal family, the same family as the Buddha's birth family. When she reached adulthood, she was one

of the future Buddha's concubines. Later she joined Mahapajapati Gotami in renunciation. The Buddha sent a vision of himself to her and used it to speak this verse. She was enlightened from hearing this verse.

6 Dhammapala says (Pruitt 1999: 19–20) that this Tissa's story is the same as the previous Tissa's; this is also the case for Dhira, Vira, Mitta, Bhadra, and Upasama, whose verses follow. All were royal concubines of the future Buddha before he set forth on his quest for enlightenment. The Buddha spoke a verse to each of them through a radiant vision that he sent to each, except for Vira who received her verse from the Buddha himself. Each of these *therīs* was enlightened when she heard her verse from the Buddha, and each repeated the verse spoken by the Buddha to her to announce her achievement.

7 P includes an additional verse here, attributed to another Dhira:

> The name you are called by means Self-reliance, Dhira,
>
> you are a nun with her sensibilities developed,
> take care of the body, it's your last,
> but make sure it doesn't become a vehicle for death after this.

8 *Bhāvitindriyā,* with sense and cognitive faculties well-cultivated.

9 Mutta was the daughter of a poor Brahman. When she had reached puberty, her parents gave her in marriage to a hunched-back Brahman. Unhappy in her life with him, she received permission from her husband to become a nun. She used this verse in her own spiritual practices. If, in meditation, her mind wandered, she said this verse to restore her concentration. She repeated the verse again when she was enlightened.

10 Dhammadinna was born in a respectable family and then was married to a wealthy merchant. Her husband went to hear the Buddha and was transformed spiritually by that experience. As a result, he wanted to be celibate. After asking Dhammadinna's own wishes, he sent her to live among the Buddha's ordained female followers. After Dhammadinna was enlightened, she returned to where her husband lived and preached the Buddha's teaching to him. The Buddha later praised her as the best among the nuns in preaching the dhamma. She spoke this verse at the time of her

enlightenment, as she reflected on the effort that she had made.

11 Dhammapala interprets "who has gone upstream" in a general sense of "up the stream of continued existence" (*saṃsārasoto*) and as one who has gone "up the stream of the path," and indicates that Dhammadinna is so spiritually advanced that she will not be reborn (Pruitt 1999: 31).

12 Dhammapala says (Pruitt 1999: 31) that Visakha's story is the same as Dhira's. This would mean that she also was a concubine of the future Buddha's. She said this verse at the time of her enlightenment not only to announce her own achievement, but also to encourage others in their efforts.

13 Dhammapala says that her story is the same as Tissa's (Pruitt 1999: 32). The Buddha sent a vision to her. It looked as if he were seated in front of her, and it spoke this verse to her. At the end of the verse, she was enlightened.

14 *Dhātuyo;* see Glossary, s.v. *Dhātu*.

15 Dhammapala says that her story is the same as Tissa's (Pruitt 1999: 33). She too was born in the Sakya royal family and was a concubine of the future Buddha's. She went forth with Mahapajapati Gotami. The Buddha spoke this verse to her in a vision and when he was finished, she was enlightened. She then repeated the verse as an account of her own experience.

16 Sumana was born as the sister of King Pasenadi, one of the great royal devotees of the Buddha. She heard the Buddha preaching a sermon to her brother and she was converted, but she waited a long time to renounce so she could take care of her grandmother. When her grandmother had died, she was already quite advanced in the stages of the Buddhist religious life because of her practice as a laywoman and to continue that practice, she asked for ordination. The Buddha, knowing her spiritual maturity, spoke this verse to her. At the end of it, she was enlightened. Sumana repeated the verse herself and then she was ordained.

17 Dhamma was born in a respectable family and was married to a suitable husband. She came to trust in the Buddha's teaching and wanted to go forth, but her husband would not allow it. Even so, she devoted herself to practicing what the Buddha taught as a laywoman, living as if she were ordained, including collecting food as alms. One day, she fell down while coming home from collecting alms and she used that mishap as a support for cultivating insight,

just like the stick she used to support her body. She was enlightened there and spoke this verse at that time.

18 Dhammapala says (Pruitt 1999: 36) that Sangha's story is the same as Dhira's. This would mean that she also was a concubine in the future Buddha's harem.

19 Dhammapala reads the singular "son" as "children."

Poems with Two Verses

1 Abhirupananda was the chief wife of one of the Sakyas, the royal family in which the Buddha was born. She was called "beautiful Nanda" because of her physical beauty. On the evening before her wedding, her fiancé died, and her parents then made her go forth as a renunciant. Even though she was ordained, she was still conceited about her looks. She avoided going near the Buddha because she expected him to disparage physical beauty. The Buddha, knowing this, demanded that she come before him. When she did come before him, the Buddha created an image of a beautiful woman and then showed the same woman decrepit with age. Nanda was afraid of what she realized was inevitable for her own body and the Buddha then spoke this verse to her. Nanda attained enlightenment when he was finished and she repeated these verses herself.

2 Dhammapala says that Jenta's story is similar to Abhirupananda's (Pruitt 1999: 41). Jenta was born in the family of the king of the Licchavis, a powerful Kshatriya group at the time of the Buddha. Jenta was enlightened when she heard the Buddha preach and she spoke these verses at the end of his sermon.

Reading her name as Jentī (i.e., Jayantī), "Victorious," as attested in P is appropriate to her attainments, as Wright (1999: 521) has pointed out.

3 The constituent factors of enlightenment.

4 Sumangala's mother was born in a poor family. Her first son was Sumangala and that is how she became known only as "Sumangala's mother." Her son went forth first, and he became enlightened. She later went forth, and one day she remembered all the bad things she had been released from as a result of her ordination. This incited her to make even greater efforts in her spiritual life. She spoke these verses when she was enlightened.

5 Addhakasi was born in the family of a rich merchant in Benares, but when she grew up, she became a prostitute. Dhammapala

attributes this turn of events to her calling a nun a prostitute in a previous life at the time of another Buddha (Pruitt 1999: 45). It was the resulting karma that caused her to become a prostitute. Eventually, when she was older, she went forth among nuns, and she said these verses when she was enlightened.

6 "Half-kasi" is literal meaning of the name Aḍḍhakāsi; it also means "inhabitant of rich Kasi."

7 *Tisso vijjā;* see introduction and Glossary about *tevijjā*.

8 Chitta was born in a rich family. After seeing the Buddha and gaining faith in him, she was ordained by Mahapajapati Gotami. When she was very old, she went to practice away from others in the forest. The verses were spoken at the time that she was enlightened.

9 Mettika was born in a wealthy family. Dhammapala says that her story is similar to Chitta's. She too went to a mountain to engage in religious practices away from others in her old age. She spoke these verses at the time she was enlightened.

10 *Tisso vijjā;* see introduction and Glossary about *tevijjā*.

11 Mitta was born in the Sakya royal family in which the Buddha was born. She was ordained by Mahapajapati Gotami, and through her own strenuous efforts, she became enlightened after only a short time. These verses were spoken when she looked back at what she had accomplished and express her happiness about her achievement.

12 One of four days each month marking a stage of the moon's waxing and waning, a day of religious observances in Buddhist communities.

13 Abhaya's mother was a prostitute in the town of Ujjeni. King Bimbasara, one of the Buddha's great royal devotees and a friend of the Buddha, had heard about her beauty and her other good qualities and decided that he wanted to see her for himself. Bimbasara slept with her for one night. She became pregnant, however, and when she told the king about her pregnancy, he asked that if the child were a son that the boy be sent to him when he had grown. She called her son "Abhaya," and when he was seven, she sent him to the king; he was raised from then on as a prince. Abhaya eventually became a Buddhist monk, and when his mother heard her son preach, she was enlightened quickly after that. After she was enlightened, her son spoke these verses to her in the manner

of a teaching. She then repeated them herself as an expression of her achievement.

14 Abhaya was born in a respectable family in Ujjeni. She went forth out of affection for the monk Abhaya's mother. One day while she was using something foul as the object of her meditation, the Buddha appeared to her in a vision and taught her how to meditate by contemplating a corpse as it decomposed. He then spoke these two verses to her. At the end of the verses, Abhaya was enlightened and repeated them herself.

15 Sama was born in a wealthy family and as a young woman, she became the close friend of another woman named Samavati. Samavati died, and Sama could not get over her grief for her. When she heard Ananda, the beloved disciple of the Buddha, preach, she began to have insight into the nature of things and very quickly became enlightened. When she looked back at what she had accomplished, she spoke these verses.

Poems with Three Verses

1 This Sama was born in a respectable family, and she too was a friend of Samavati (see vv. 37–38). The latter's death moved her to go forth, but for twenty-five years, she advanced very little spiritually. When she was an old woman, she was taught by the Buddha himself and she then quickly attained enlightenment. When she did, she spoke these verses.

2 The Buddha.

3 Uttama was born in the family of a wealthy merchant. As a young adult, she heard Patachara preach, and she was motivated by that to go forth. She made some spiritual progress, but could not become enlightened. When Patachara saw this, she gave Uttama further instructions, and by following what Patachara said, Uttama did become enlightened. When Uttama looked back at what she had accomplished, she spoke these verses.

4 This verse employs Buddhist technical vocabulary that is used to describe the objective nature of a person: ***khanda,*** the five aggregates (constituents of a person), ***dhātu,*** the basic elements that make up everything, and ***āyatana,*** a concept that holds together the internal and external bases of sensory experience, namely, the senses and the objects of the senses.

5 That is, nibbana.

6 Dantika was the daughter of a Brahman who was the chief minister for the king of Kosala. As a young adult, she converted to Buddhism when she saw the Jetavana monastery given to the Buddha by the king. Later she was ordained by Mahapajapati Gotami. She once saw someone mounting an elephant, and while meditating on that, she became enlightened. She explained what happened in these verses.

7 Ubbiri was born in a wealthy family. She was very beautiful and the king of Kosala made her a part of his harem. She had a daughter with the king, and she was named Jivanti. The king made Ubbiri a queen because of his happiness about the birth of that daughter, but the daughter died as a child. Ubbiri, in her grief, went to the cemetery every day, but no matter where she was, she always lamented over her daughter's death. The Buddha sent her a vision of himself that spoke the first verse to her. That helped her to see how the Buddha's teaching applied to her particular situation, and she began to practice what the Buddha taught. When she became enlightened, she spoke the next two verses.

8 The name of her deceased daughter, which literally means "life."

9 The monastic community established by the Buddha.

10 Sukka was born in a wealthy family. As a young adult, she became a lay follower of the Buddha. When she heard the *therī* Dhammadinna preach, she decided to ordain with that nun and after a very short time, she was enlightened. Sukka herself gained a following of five hundred nuns and was considered to be a great teacher. One day when she was preaching to her followers, a god (*devatā*) who lived in a tree nearby was able to hear and was pleased with her. That god went into Rajagaha and praised Sukka throughout the city by saying the first two verses. Sukka said the last verse at the time of her death.

11 Sela was the daughter of the king of Alavika. She saw the Buddha as a child with her father and became a lay follower of the Buddha. Later she ordained, and she became enlightened after only a short time. After her enlightenment, Mara came to her in the form of a stranger, and said the first verse in an effort to undermine her. When Sela heard what he said, she thought that Mara was a fool who could not see what she had accomplished, and she spoke her verses to make him understand and also to frighten him.

A different set of verses is attributed to Sela in the

Bhikkhunīsaṃyutta of the *Saṃyuttanikāya;* see S I.134 and Bodhi 2000: 228–229. As the notes to the text indicate, some of the verses attributed here to Sela are attributed to a nun named Alavika in the *Bhikkhunīsaṃyutta*.

Mara is a figure of Buddhist mythology, superhuman in powers and the personification of evil; he is a tempter to those striving for the freedom achieved by the way of life taught by the Buddha.

12 Soma was the daughter of the chief minister of King Bimbasara, a great devotee of the Buddha and also the Buddha's friend. As a young adult, she became a lay follower of the Buddha and then later ordained. She became enlightened after only a short time. After that, she enjoyed the happiness of the freedom that enlightenment gives. One day she went into the forest to rest at midday and Mara, invisible, approached her. He spoke the first verse from up in the air in an attempt to undermine her religious practice. Soma rejected what Mara said and then spoke the next two verses.

A series of verses overlapping with these are attributed to Soma in the *Bhikkhunīsaṃyutta;* see S I.129 and Bodhi 2000: 222–223.

A Poem with Four Verses

1 Bhadda Kapilani was born in a Brahman clan and was given in marriage to Pipphali Kumara, also a Brahman; her husband would later become the *thera* Mahakassapa. Together, she and her husband became renunciants among non-Buddhist ascetics. After five years with them, Bhadda Kapilani ordained with Mahapajapati Gotami. Very shortly after that, she was enlightened. Bhadda Kapilani was said by the Buddha to be foremost among those who could remember their previous existences. In her verses, Bhadda Kapilani first praises the good qualities and achievements of her former husband, Kassapa, and then speaks about herself.

2 In Hinduism, some Brahmans are said to have erudition because of their knowledge of three Vedas, but here, Kassapa is praised as a real Brahman because he knows the three things that most people don't know.

Poems with Five Verses

1 This nun was Mahapajapati's nurse and served her, but Dhammapala says that her ancestry was not known (Pruitt 1999: 99). She ordained with Mahapajapati Gotami, but for twenty-five

years she was assailed by urges for sensual pleasures, to her great frustration. She became a follower of the *therī* Dhammadinna and heard her preach. A short time after that, she gained such powers as the six higher knowledges (see Glossary, s.v. *Chaḷabhiññā*). She spoke these verses at the time of attaining these powers.

2 See the note to v. 43.

3 *Chaḷabhiññā;* see Glossary.

4 Vimala was the daughter of a woman who made her living from her beauty, and Vimala did the same. One day she saw one of the Buddha's chief disciples, Moggallana, collecting alms and she tried to seduce him. Sometimes it is said that she was prompted to do this by members of an ascetic group that was a rival of the Buddha's community. In response to her efforts at seduction, Moggallana spoke some verses to her about the foulness of the body; these verses are included in the *Theragāthā* (vv. 1150–1153) and are quoted in Dhammapala's commentary. They end with this verse:

> If any person knew you as I know you, he would avoid you,
> keeping far away, as one avoids a cess pit in the rainy season.
> (Pruitt 1999: 101)

When Vimala heard what Moggallana said in reaction at her efforts to seduce him, she was ashamed. She also gained faith in the Buddha's teachings and ordained. Once she was enlightened, she spoke her verses, as she looked back at how she came to her enlightenment.

5 Siha was named after her uncle, a general named Siha. As a young adult, she first heard the dhamma when it was preached to her uncle. She received permission from her parents to be ordained. She did not make much progress in meditation, as she was distracted by her own thoughts. Out of frustration with herself, she decided to commit suicide, but the moment when she had put a noose around her neck, she attained enlightenment. At that moment her mind was freed, the noose fell off her neck. She then spoke her verses.

6 *Kilesa;* see Glossary.

7 Sundarinanda was born in the Sakya royal family. She was named Nanda, but because of her looks, she was called "Beautiful Nanda" (*sundarīnanda*). Imitating others in her own family who had

ordained as followers of the Buddha, such as the Buddha's son Rahula and his stepmother Mahapajapati Gotami, who was her own mother, she joined the Buddha's monastic order. She did so, however, imitating others, not out of personal faith of her own. She was still conceited about her beauty. Like Abhirupananda, she avoided going before the Buddha because she expected him to disparage physical beauty. Eventually she did come before the Buddha. Like Abhirupananda, the Buddha showed her an image, and this one was of a young woman gradually becoming old. Sundarinanda then began to meditate on what this suggested, and the Buddha spoke the first three verses as instruction for her. He instructed her further on the nature of our bodies, and eventually she was enlightened. She spoke the final verses at the time of her enlightenment.

8 Nanduttara was born in a Brahman family. She first went forth as a Jain, and like Bhadda Kundalakesa, she wandered across India in search of people who would debate religious topics with her. One debate was with one of the Buddha's two chief disciples, Moggallana. He defeated her in debate, and she converted to Buddhism. She became enlightened very shortly after joining the Buddhist community of nuns. She spoke her verses at the time of her enlightenment.

9 Mittakali was born in a Brahman family. She heard the Buddha preach when she was a young adult and joined his monastic community at that time. She was more concerned about being honored by others, however, than actual practice and thus she achieved little from her life as an ascetic. Eventually, she began to understand that death is inevitable in life, and she began to practice to gain insight rather than to get recognition. After a short time, she was able to attain enlightenment and it was then that she said her verses.

10 *Khanda;* see Glossary.

11 Sakula was born in a Brahman family. Witnessing the Buddha accept the Jetavana monastery, she was converted to Buddhism. Later she heard the dhamma preached by an enlightened monk and she ordained. After a very short time, she was enlightened. The Buddha placed her foremost among those who can see what is invisible.

12 Sona was born in a respectable family. She had ten sons and one

daughter after she married. When her husband went forth, she raised her children alone. When they were adults, she divided the family property among her children, keeping none for herself. Her children began to mistreat her, and she could not understand how they had come to despise her. That is when she approached a community of Buddhist nuns and asked for ordination. Once she became a nun, she did various penitential practices very seriously. The Buddha knew her capability and sent a vision to her and spoke a verse that is now in the *Dhammapada* (verse 115):

> Should one live a hundred years
> Not seeing dhamma supreme;
> Better still is one day lived
> Of one seeing dhamma supreme.
> (Carter and Palihawadana 2000: 22)

Sona attained enlightenment when she heard this verse. The Buddha placed Sona as foremost among those who make an effort in religious practice. She said her verse on an occasion when she was recollecting her achievements.

13 This verse employs Buddhist technical vocabulary that is used to describe the objective nature of a person: *khanda,* the five aggregates (constituents of a person), *dhātu,* the basic elements that make up everything, and *āyatana,* a concept that holds together the internal and external bases of sensory experience, namely, the senses and the objects of the senses. See Glossary.

14 *Khanda*; see Glossary.

15 Bhadda Kundalakesi was the daughter of a wealthy merchant. She was given all that she could have wanted, but it was not enough. One day from her grilled window, she saw a convicted thief named Sattuka being led to his execution. She fell in love with him and told her father that she could not live without him. Her father was able to get the thief released through bribery and he came to live with Bhadda, who waited on him devotedly. After living with Bhadda a short while, Sattuka wanted her ornaments for himself and devised a plot to rob her. She saw through his scheme and used her wits to kill him. She knew that she could not go home after murdering her husband, so she ordained as a Jain nun. Her hair grew back quickly after it was removed in the ordination ritual, and when it grew

back it was curly. As a result Bhadda became known as "Bhadda Kundalakesi" ("Curly-locks Bhadda"). She wandered India looking for people to debate with. At one point, she had a debate with Sariputta, one of the two chief disciples of the Buddha, in front of a large crowd. She was defeated in the debate and converted to Buddhism. Sariputta sent her to the Buddha to take refuge before him and the Buddha spoke a verse of the *Dhammapada* (v. 101) to her:

> Though a thousand be the verses
> With words of no avail,
> Better is a single line of verse,
> Having heard which, one is pacified.
> (Carter and Palihawadana 2000: 20)

Bhadda Kundalakesi attained enlightenment when she heard this verse and she immediately asked the Buddha for ordination. She spoke the first five of her verses at a later time when she recollected her attainments. The final verse she spoke when a lay follower gave her his own robe.

16 Dhammapala interprets these practices in the context of Bhadda's experience among Jains earlier (*pubbe nigaṇṭhī hutvā*), and he then interprets the ascetic practices named more narrowly: plucking out the hair, not cleaning the teeth, and wearing only one robe.

17 *Puñña;* see Glossary.

18 Patachara's story is one of the most famous in the Theravadin world and versions of it are found in the commentary on the *Dhammapada* and the commentary on the *Anguttaranikāya* section of the Pali canon.

Patachara was born in the family of a wealthy merchant. When she was a young adult, she had an affair with a servant in the household and, although he was an unsuitable partner, she ran away with him. Eventually she became pregnant and wanted to return home to give birth in her family's home. She did not reach their house before her labor began, and she gave birth on the roadside. When she became pregnant a second time, she again wanted to return home. Again, her labor began before she reached there and she gave birth on the roadside, this time in the middle of a violent rainstorm. Her husband died of a snakebite trying to build a shelter to protect her. She tried to continue on to her parent's home. Her first child and the newborn died as she tried to cross a river flooded by the rain. When she approached her parent's village, she learned that her whole family had died when their house had collapsed in the storm. She became mad with grief. It was only when she came near the Buddha that her grief ended; he was able to pierce the madness of grief and restore Patachara to her senses. The Buddha then began to teach her his dhamma. One day, while she was meditating, she saw water "running" over the dry sand, some being absorbed quickly, some a little longer, and some after that. She saw that what happened with humans, each of whom have different lengths of life, is not different than what happened with the water. One night, she entered her room and as she was extinguishing her lamp to go to sleep, it gave her an insight into how to become free. She attained enlightenment, but she remembered the stages of her efforts to do so in her verses.

19 These followers of Patachara were all born in good families but in different places. Each heard Patachara preach when they were young adults and this motivated each of them to ordain.

20 *Tevijjamha;* see Glossary, s.v. *Tevijjā*.

21 Chanda was born in a Brahman family. Her family became impoverished by the time she had become a young adult and the family was reduced to a life of misery. All of Chanda's relatives died in a cholera epidemic. Without the aid of any relative, Chanda became destitute, homeless, and survived by begging on the street when she met Patachara and ordained because she saw it as a way of getting food. After ordination, however, she followed Patachara's instruction and quickly became enlightened. She spoke her verses after looking back over her accomplishments.

22 *Tevijjamhi;* see Glossary, s.v. *Tevijjā*.

Poems with Six Verses

1 These women were all born in good families in different places. All of them had dead children, and all of them were unable to overcome their grief for those children. Patachara, who had also lost her own children, was able to dispel their grief through her teaching.

2 The monastic community established by the Buddha.

3 Vasetthi was born into a respectable family in Vesali. She had a

son with her husband, but the son died as a child. Overwhelmed by her grief, Vasetthi went mad. She ran away from home, and wandered, becoming homeless. The very sight of the Buddha, whom she saw as he went down the street, dispelled her madness. The Buddha taught her with a brief sermon and she requested ordination right after that. She spoke her verses after she became enlightened, looking back at her life.

4 An epithet of the Buddha, literally "the Well-Gone One."

5 Gotama is the clan name of the family into which the Buddha was born.

6 Khema was born in the royal family of the kingdom of Madda. She was very beautiful. When she became an adult, she was sent to live in the harem of King Bimbisara, the great devotee and friend of the Buddha. When the Buddha was living in a monastery nearby, Khema did not want to go see him because she expected the Buddha to rebuke her for her conceit over her beauty. King Bimbisara ordered that she be made to see the Buddha, even if had to be done forcibly. This turned out to be the case, but when she was brought before the Buddha, she quickly had a conversion experience. The Buddha spoke a verse from the *Dhammapada* (347) to her, and at the end of the verse, she was transformed spiritually in a significant way. (Dhammapala is aware of different accounts of what happened and he notes that some say that she was enlightened, while others say that she only entered the stream to enlightenment.)

The Buddha described Khema as foremost among the nuns that have great wisdom.

Her poem is a dialogue between her and Mara who sought to seduce her with promises of sexual pleasure.

See Glossary, s.v. Mara. Here Mara has assumed another bodily appearance.

7 Referring to making fire oblations.

8 Sujata was the daughter of a wealthy merchant, and her parents arranged a marriage for her with the son of an equally wealthy merchant. She enjoyed a happy marriage with him. After enjoying a seasonal festival, she had the chance to see the Buddha. The Buddha preached a sermon to her and she became enlightened right there. After enlightenment, she obtained permission from both her parents and her husband to ordain, and she spoke her

verses at the time of her going forth.

9 *Tisso vijjā;* see Glossary, s.v. *Tevijjā.*

10 Anopama was the daughter of a wealthy merchant, and she was called "Incomparable" (anopama) because of her beauty. When she had reached an age appropriate for marriage, there were many men of high social standing—merchants' sons, princes, ministers' sons—who asked to marry her, but she had her mind set on renunciation. She made great spiritual progress as a layperson and then asked the Buddha to be ordained. He sent her to the nuns' monastery for ordination, and seven days after her ordination, she became enlightened.

11 Mahapajapati Gotami was the younger sister of the Buddha's mother, Mahamaya. Both sisters were married to King Suddhodana, the Buddha's father. She raised the future Buddha after his mother died in childbirth. Mahapajapati Gotami requested ordination from the Buddha a number of times, but he was reluctant to ordain women. The Buddha did finally relent and Mahapajapati Gotami was the first woman that he ordained; the story of how she finally was given ordination and what this entailed for her and for the Buddha's heritage is an important story throughout the Buddhist world and has also been subject to considerable scholarship; see, for example, Wijayaratna 2010: 9–20 and Collett 2013: chapter 1.

12 In Buddhist discourse, "Buddha" is an epithet of someone who is enlightened through his own effort and who teaches others; in English, we can say "the Buddha" to refer to Gotama, while "a Buddha" or "Buddhas" refers to those who reach this achievement. The translation follows Dhammapala in taking the compound *buddhavīra* to refer to the general category.

13 The Buddha as personal lord.

14 Gutta was the daughter of a Brahman. As a young adult, she was already disgusted with lay life and, with the permission of her parents, was ordained by Mahapajapati Gotami. Although she made great efforts, she was unable to master meditation because her mind tended to wander. The Buddha first spoke these verses to her to encourage her in her efforts at meditation.

15 Vijaya was a friend of Khema's when both were householders. When she heard that Khema had ordained, Vijaya felt that she should do so too. Khema, sensing her inclination, instructed her in the dhamma, and this helped Vijaya to decide to go forth. She

attained enlightenment shortly after ordination, and she spoke her poem at that occasion.

Different verses are attributed to a nun also named Vijaya in the *Bhikkhunīsaṃyutta;* see S I.130–131 and Bodhi 2000: 224–225.

16 *Indriyāni,* the cognitive faculties of a person.

Poems with Seven Verses

1 When Uttara was a young adult, she approached Patachara, and that nun preached to her. She decided to pursue the path to enlightenment and ordained. Once ordained, she was further instructed by Patachara, attaining enlightenment after a short time.

2 *Tevijjā;* see Glossary.

3 The chief of the gods.

4 Chala was the daughter of a Brahman. Her younger sisters were Upachala and Sisupachala, both of whose verses are also found in the *Therīgāthā*. They were all the younger sisters of Sariputta, one of the two chief disciples of the Buddha. Sariputta inspired them to go forth, and they left the household life. Their families were heartbroken. After ordination, each made every effort in her practice, and all attained enlightenment quickly.

Mara tried to seduce Chala with promises of sexual pleasure, to great failure. Chala's poem is the dialogue between her and Mara.

Verses quite similar to Chala's are attributed to Sisupachala in the *Bhikkhunīsaṃyutta;* see S I.133 and Bodhi 2000: 228.

5 *Bhāvitindriyā,* with cognitive faculties well-cultivated.

6 That is, the four noble truths.

7 *Tisso vijjā*; see Glossary, s.v. *Tevijjā*.

8 Upachala was the sister of Chala; both were sisters of Sisupachala and Sariputta. Dhammapala says that Upachala's story was like the story of Chala.

9 *Bhāvitindriyā,* with cognitive faculties well-cultivated.

10 The four noble truths.

11 *Tisso vijjā;* see Glossary, s.v. *Tevijjā*.

A Poem with Eight Verses

1 Sisupachala was the sister of Chala; both were sisters of Upachala and Sariputta. Dhammapala says that Sisupachala's story was the same as the story of Chala.

Verses quite similar to some of Sisupachala's are attributed to Upachala in the *Bhikkhunīsaṃyutta;* see S I.133 and Bodhi 2000: 227.

2 *Indriyesu,* the cognitive faculties.

3 Higher realms in Buddhist cosmology, all characterized by greater power and pleasure than is found among humans and realms of rebirth below humans. These five realms are all realms of gods in the *kamaloka,* the sensuous world, and thus they are not the highest realms of divine pleasure in the Buddhist cosmos.

4 *Tisso vijjā;* see Glossary, s.v. *Tevijjā.*

A Poem with Nine Verses

1 Vaddha's mother was born in a respectable family. She gave birth to Vaddha after her marriage and from then on, she was called "Vaddha's mother." She had a conversion experience after hearing a monk preach. She left her son in the care of relatives and went to the nuns' monastery and ordained. Vaddha himself ordained and he went to the nuns' monastery specifically to show himself to his mother. When Vaddha's mother asked him why he had come, she said the first verses to him.

All of vv. 204–212 are attributed to Vaddha's mother, but Dhammapala recognized that some of the verses (vv. 207, 210–212) were spoken by Vaddha to his mother. He explained "she herself repeated the verses spoken by him. In that way, the verses came to be called the therī's." (Pruitt 1999: 221.)

Winternitz suggests that these verses in the *Therīgāthā* and the verses attributed to Vaddha in the *Theragāthā* (vv. 335–339) were originally one narrative poem that was subsequently divided somewhat carelessly between the two anthologies (Winternitz 1987: 101).

Vaddha's verses included in the *Theragāthā* are:

My mother drove me forward well,
and having heard what she said,
instructed by my mother,
I became full of energy and resolute,
I attained enlightenment.

I am enlightened and worthy of offerings,
I know the three things that most don't know

and I have seen the deathless,
Having conquered Mara's army,
I live free of all that defiles from within.

All those things that once defiled me, whether inside or out,
they are all gone, without exception,
and they will not appear again.

The sister knew what she was talking about
when she spoke about this,
Maybe now there is no lust in you.

Suffering is ended, this is the last body,
there will not be another existence,
one that brings with it birth, death, and samsara.

2 The participles here are in a masculine form, which would be unproblematic if the verse was spoken by Vaddha. The translation here follows Dhammapala, who attributes the verse to Vaddha's mother and converts the masculine forms to feminine in his commentary.

3 *Tisso vijjā;* see Glossary, s.v. *Tevijjā.*

A Poem with Eleven Verses

1 Kisagotami's story is also one of the most famous in the Theravada Buddhist world, found for example in the commentary on the *Dhammapada,* and various versions of her story differ in details from what is found in Dhammapala's commentary on the *Therīgāthā.*

Dhammapala says that Kisagotami was born in a poor family. When she was married, her husband's family treated her badly, looking down on her because she came from a poor family. They felt more favorable toward her when she gave birth to a son. That son died as a child and Kisagotami became mad with grief. Carrying her son's body, she went about asking everyone for medicine for her son, not able to take in the reality of her son's death. Eventually, she came before the Buddha and also asked him for medicine to cure her dead son. The Buddha told her that he could make such a medicine and instructed her to bring mustard seed from a house where no one has ever died that he would use in preparing the remedy. She went from house to house looking for such a residence so that she could get the necessary mustard seed. She quickly realized that every house had more deaths than could be counted, and this restored her back to her normal mind. She also realized that the Buddha foresaw that this would happen for her, and did what he did out of kindness and sympathy for her. Kisagotami became a nun, and with the aid of further instruction from the Buddha, she became enlightened. When later the Buddha praised Kisagotami for her willingness to wear rough robes, Kisagotami reflected that she had attained all that she had through the support of the Buddha. At that point, she spoke her verses in praise of the virtuous state of being a good friend (*kalyāṇamittatā*), such as the Buddha had been to her.

A different set of verses is attributed to Kisagotami in the *Bhikkhunīsaṃyutta* of the *Saṃyuttanikāya;* see S I.129 and Bodhi 2000: 223–224.

2 That is, one should know the four noble truths.

A Poem with Twelve Verses

1 Uppalavanna's poem is one of the most difficult to understand in the *Therīgāthā,* and Dhammapala's commentary is not helpful in getting any sense of how it should be taken as a whole.

The story of Uppalavanna's previous lives is the most elaborate one that Dhammapala tells in his commentary on the *Therīgāthā,* and the account of Uppalavanna in the canonical *Apadāna* that Dhammapala includes in his commentary is equally elaborate. The *Apadāna* says that Uppalavanna and other nuns whose poems are included in the *Therīgāthā,* such as Khema, Patachara, Kundala, Kisagotami, Dhammadinna, and Visakha, were all sisters; it also says that Uppalavanna and Rahula, the Buddha's son, were brother and sister in a previous life. How these various stories of the past illuminate the verses of Uppalavanna is unclear.

Dhammapala divides Uppalavanna's poem into four parts (224–226; 227–228; 229; 230–235), but he gives no clear guidance on how the four parts should be connected together. Norman (2007: 122) suggests that this is a case of "verses uttered at different times [which] have been collected together with no attempt made to produce an organic whole."

Dhammapala suggests that the two verses in the first part of the poem were recited by Uppalavanna on an occasion of spiritual turmoil arising from a fear of the inevitable, but they were not autobiographical. Uppalavanna simply made the verses first said by others into an expression of her own inner state arising from her seeing the dangers brought by sexual urges. Dhammapala suggests that the verses are connected with the cowives—mother and daughter—of the Thera Gangatiriya; verses attributed to him are found in the *Theragāthā* (vv. 127–128).

Dhammapala says that vv. 227 and 228 were said on another occasion when Uppalavanna reviewed her own accomplishments.

Verse 229, according to Dhammapala, was said when Uppalavanna made a chariot with her special powers and used it to go the Buddha at the time of the Buddha's performance of the twin miracle.

Verses 230–235 are an encounter between Uppalavanna and Mara, similar to the set of poems attributed to different nuns and found in the *Bhikkhunīsaṃyutta*.

Verses that overlap with these are attributed to Uppalavanna in the *Bhikkhunīsaṃyutta;* see S I.131–132 and Bodhi 2000: 225–226.

2 *Chaḷabhiññā;* see Glossary.

3 Cha . . . abhiññā; see Glossary, s.v. Chaḷabhiññā.

A Poem with Sixteen Verses

1 Punna was born as a servant in the house of the merchant Anathapindaka, one of the great devotees of the Buddha. As a laywoman, she became a "stream-winner," and thus entered the higher states toward enlightenment. After she converted the Brahman, as described in her poem, Anathapindaka made her a free woman and she ordained, quickly attaining enlightenment after that.

2 *Tevijjo;* see Glossary, s.v. *Tevijjā*.

3 There is word play here on the word *nhātako* (Skt. *snātaka*), which is the term applied to a Brahman who has performed the ritual bath at the end of his Vedic studentship.

Poems with about Twenty Verses

1 Ambapali is said to have born spontaneously at the foot of a mango (*amba*) tree in a royal garden at Vesali, as the result of a

determination she had made in her previous life because of disgust with the condition of being an embryo. The royal gardener saw her and took her home. She was beautiful; when she grew up many princes desired her to be their wife, and they quarreled among themselves. The judges who settled their quarrel made her into a prostitute, saying "let her belong to everyone" (Pruitt 1999: 260). As a laywoman, she converted to Buddhism and made many offerings to the Buddha and his monastic order. Her own son, Vimala Kondañña, preached a sermon to her, and she went forth. She spoke her verses in her old age and later, when she had become enlightened, repeated them again.

2 As Norman notes, it does not seem that *uttamaṅgajo* can be correct. He suggests "that we punctuate *uttam'aṅg'abhu,* and assume *abhu* is a mistake for *ahu,* or more likely a genuine historical development < Skt *abhūt,*" and his suggested punctuation is followed in the translation here (Norman 2007: 132).

3 *Āyatā,* large or "long" in length.

4 Reading *saṇhatuṅgasadisī* as a *dvandva* compound, as Dhammapala does. Norman 2007: 135, while acknowledging that Dhammapala's interpretation is "quite possible," suggests that "since in every other occurrence of *sadisa-* in this poem a comparison is made, ... on the grounds of style we must assume that a simile is intended here," and thus he translates *saṇhatuṅgasadisī* as "my nose looked beautiful like a delicate peak."

5 The form and meaning of *upakūlitā* is uncertain; see Norman 2007: 136. The translation here follows Dhammapala's gloss.

6 That is, ash-colored and scabrous.

7 *Thevikīva* here is problematic, as equally are the readings found in other witnesses; see Norman 2007: 140. The translation here follows Dhammapala's gloss.

8 The translation reflects the pun in *apalepapatito* that is suggested in Gombrich 1990, with *avalalepa,* a phonetic variant in Pali for *apalepa,* meaning "pride, haughtiness," as well as "plaster."

9 Rohini was born in the family of a rich Brahman. As a young adult, she heard the Buddha preach and became a "stream-winner," thus progressing toward enlightenment. She herself preached to her parents, on the basis of what she had heard, and converted them. She asked for their permission to ordain and then very quickly became enlightened. When she was enlightened, she repeated

verses that were a dialogue between her and her father at the time when she had just become a stream-winner. She was a great teacher in the women's monastic community and had many followers.

10 Greed, anger, and delusion.

11 Dhammapala explains that these are good mental states.

12 Although prepared for another purpose, the food, etc., is available as alms.

13 Chapa was born the daughter of a chief deer hunter. When the ascetic Upaka came to her village, Chapa's father asked her to attend to his needs. When the ascetic saw Chapa's beauty, he was overcome by his sexual urges and eventually felt that the only thing he wanted was to have Chapa. Chapa and Upaka lived together, with Upaka being a meat carrier for the hunters of the village. Chapa belittled Upaka in her lullabies to their son, mocking that he was only a meat-carrier, and eventually Upaka wanted to leave her and go back to being an ascetic. In fact, he wanted to ordain in the monastic order of the Buddha, having met the Buddha before he had come to Chapa's village. This he set out to do, one day, out of anger at Chapa. When Upaka departed, Chapa was heartbroken. She left their son with her father and followed Upaka, eventually ordaining among the female followers of the Buddha. When she was enlightened, she spoke verses of a dialogue between her and Upaka as her *udāna*.

14 Benares.

15 The translation reflects the polysemy in *amatam,* as *a-mata,* deathless, and as *amata,* ambrosial.

16 That is, the four noble truths.

17 Chapa's husband gives the merit of these actions to her, a common feature of Buddhist rituals where the good results of an action are transferred to another; see Glossary, s.v. *Tevijjā.*

18 *Tisso vijjā;* see Glossary, s.v. *Tevijjā.*

19 Sundari was born in Benares, the daughter of a Brahman. When she was a young adult, her younger brother died. Her father was overwhelmed with grief. He met the *therī* Vasetthi and in the first two verses, asked her how to overcome his grief. Vasetthi replies in her own verses, explaining her own freedom from grief. When Sundari's father heard that, he asked her how she had been able to gain that freedom, and Vasetthi sent him to see the Buddha. The Buddha preached to him, and shortly after that, Sundari's father

ordained and quickly became enlightened. When Sundari heard her father had gone forth, she asked her mother for permission to do so too. After ordination and through her efforts, she became enlightened. After she had attained enlightenment, she went and displayed her accomplishments to the Buddha. Her mother, other relatives, and others, seeing this, were all moved to go forth themselves. Later, looking back over her accomplishments, she spoke the verses in dialogue as an expression of her achievements.

The dialogue begins with Sundari's father addressing a woman named Vasetthi at the time of the death of Sundari's younger brother. Dhammapala takes the Vasetthi addressed in these verses to be the same as the *therī* of vv. 133–138. Norman, however, takes Vasetthi as merely a clan name, and interprets the verses as a dialogue between a husband and his wife; see Norman 2007: 151.

20 Dhammapala explains that to say a mother has eaten her child is a popular but abusive idiom to find fault with a woman whose child died in childbirth.

21 The idea is that as an enlightened person she remembers the children who had died in her previous lives (Pruitt 1999: 294).

22 The Buddha as personal lord.

23 That is, he taught the four noble truths.

24 Sundari's father.

25 *Tisso vijjā;* see Glossary, s.v. *Tevijjā.*

26 Addressing the charioteer who had brought Sujata to Mithila.

27 *Tisso vijjā;* see Glossary, s.v. *Tevijjā.*

28 *Tisso vijjā;* see Glossary, s.v. *Tevijjā.*

29 An idiom that indicates a public display of spiritual achievements.

30 Sundari addresses the Buddha as "Brahman" to praise him. In Buddhist usage, "Brahman" can be used as a synonym for an arhat, someone enlightened, and thus worthy of worship.

31 Subha was the daughter of a goldsmith. She was called "Subha" because she was beautiful. As a young adult, she became a follower of the Buddha after seeing him when he came to Rajagaha, where she was living. She became a stream-winner as a layperson, after hearing the Buddha teach. Later, dissatisfied with lay life, she was ordained by Mahapajapati Gotami, the Buddha's stepmother. Although she was happy and virtuous as a nun, her relatives continually tried to seduce her back to lay life with enticements of wealth and pleasure. On one occasion, she preached to them

about the dangers of the things with which they were trying to entice her, and she was able to stop them from trying to get her to become a layperson again. Concentrating on her religious practices after that, she quickly became enlightened. The final verses of her poem were spoken by the Buddha to praise her to monks and then by Sakka, who spoke after he heard the Buddha praise her.

32 *Duggati* are the realms of misery in which rebirth can take place in Buddhist cosmology. They are in various hells, among animals, and among ghosts who coexist with humans in this world.

33 *Sukkapakkha* is the bright half of a month and thus is a time of good opportunities. Dhammapala takes the compound *sukkapakkhavisosakā,* however, as referring to a group of people (*sukkapakkha*) and glosses the word as "causing the destruction (*vināsakā*) of an irreproachable group of beings" (Pruitt 1999: 308).

34 There is a play on words with Subha's name, which means beautiful, by noting how she is *sobhaṇā,* beautiful.

35 *Tevijjā;* see Glossary.

A Poem with about Thirty Verses

1 Subha was born in a wealthy Brahman family in Rajagaha. She was beautiful and thus she was given the name Subha. She became a follower of the Buddha after seeing him on one occasion when he came to Rajagaha. She later was ordained by Mahapajapati Gotami, the Buddha's stepmother, and she quickly made progress toward becoming enlightened. One day a young man saw her going to the forest to rest at midday. Infatuated, he followed and tried to seduce her.

The story of the young rake's attempt to seduce Subha might be compared to Ravana's attempt to seduce Sita in the Ramayana, Book 3.44–45.

2 Epithet of the Buddha, literally, "Well-Gone One."

3 There is a double meaning in *tapaṇīyakatā,* "made of gleaming gold." The word also means something that is suitable for asceticism, and thus Subha is described as "a young daughter suited for asceticism," as well as like a "doll of gleaming gold."

4 Like a nymph in the park of the Tavatimsa heaven.

5 Made of fine muslin from Benares. Subha is actually wearing robes sewn from rags.

6 A being who, in Sanskrit literature, is generally conceived as being

half human and half horse, while in Pali literature, a *kinnari* is half human and half bird. In both instances, however, male *kinnaras* and female *kinnaris* are idealized as lovers, ever devoted to each other and living lives of pleasure. *Kinnaris* are also noted for their beauty and grace and for the skill in poetry, music, and dance.

7 That is, the body is filled with the corpses of the organisms that live within the body and by those that we ingest as food or with food. Dhammapala, however, glosses *kuṇapapūramhi* to indicate that the body is filled with things like hair and dirt (Pruitt 1999: 320).

8 Norman (2007: 167) notes that Turī is found in Sanskrit as the personal name of the wife of Vasudeva, and translates "Your eyes are indeed like those of Turī."

9 The great mountain at the center of the universe.

10 Constructed (*saṅkhataṃ*) objectively, in the sense of made in dependence on other things, and also subjectively, in the sense of being subject to our mental constructions.

11 Epithet of the Buddha, literally "Well-Gone One."

12 The dart of passion.

13 This verse is filled with textual and grammatical difficulties, although the general sense is clear. Norman uses this verse as evidence that Dhammapala had an already corrupt text before him (Norman 2007: xxxv). For a discussion of the textual and grammatical difficulties of the verse, see Norman 2007: 172 and Pruitt 1999: 315, 325.

14 Dhammapala says that it is a picture of the form of a woman, and the skill of the painter may sustain the perception, "Now human beings are standing, leaning against this wall" (Pruitt 1999: 326).

15 Following Dhammapala, who explains that the little ball in a hollow is a ball of lac in the hollow of a tree (Pruitt 1999: 326).

16 It is clear that these last four verses of narration, as well as the first verse, frame the dialogue between Subha and the Rake, but Dhammapala does not actually specify this.

17 Both freed from the Rake's grasp and enlightened.

18 A Buddha's body is covered with 32 major marks and 80 minor marks that display his spiritual greatness.

A Poem with about Forty Verses

1 Isidasi was the daughter of a wealthy merchant in Ujjeni; he was

publically admired for his good qualities and his moral character. Her parents gave her in marriage to a wealthy merchant's son. She lived in his house for a month, and although she was a dutiful wife, her husband abandoned her. As her poem indicates she was then given to a succession of husbands. In great unhappiness about this state of affairs, she asked her father for permission to ordain. She was ordained by Jinadatta; Norman (2007: 186) suggests, on the basis of Jinadatta's name, that she was a Jain. She quickly became enlightened after her ordination. Later, on an occasion when she was resting with a companion, the *therī* Bodhi, she gave an account of what had happened to her that led up to her becoming a nun.

2 Pāṭaliputta was the capital of Magadha in north India and the reference to the *patali* tree in its name is because several shoots of that flowering tree appeared on the day of its foundation.

3 The goddess of wealth.

4 *Tisso vijjā;* see Glossary, s.v. *Tevijjā*.

The Great Chapter

1 Sumedha was born the daughter of a king, Koncha, in the city of Mantavati. Her parents arranged a marriage for her with Anikadatta. When she was young, she had gone to the monastery of Buddhist women, together with other princesses and servants. She heard the dhamma from those nuns and began to have faith in the Buddha's teaching. As a young adult, she set her mind on a religious life as a nun. When she overheard her parents arranging her marriage, she became determined to go forth. She had already made considerable progress toward enlightenment before she was allowed to leave her parents' house and once she ordained, she quickly became enlightened.

2 A fuller sense of *pasāditā* would suggest that Sumedha came to feel that she was taken care of, in a profound sense, in this world of suffering and thus she felt at ease; in other words, she discovered that the Buddha taught his teaching for her, no less than for anyone else.

3 That is, even though fools experience for themselves the reality of the four noble truths by experiencing suffering as a result of their desire (which the second noble truth explains as the origin of suffering), they do not see what is being taught as applying to them.

4 The six realms of rebirth in the Buddhist cosmos; the four bad places of punishment are in hell, and among animals, ghosts, and asuras, the two somewhat better are among humans and gods. Dhammapala makes it clear that it is only rarely and with difficulty that one is reborn among humans or gods (Pruitt 1999: 355).

5 The word play here on *pabbajjā* is that there is no escape from hell and no chance for Buddhist ordination for those in hell.

6 Buddhas have ten powers in terms of what they can know, ranging from knowing the facts of reality to knowing the past rebirths of all beings and knowing the causal laws of karma that structure the rebirth of beings (Pruitt 1999: 355).

7 The translation here includes the implication supplied by Dhammapala.

8 There are many difficulties and uncertainties with this verse; for a discussion of possibilities of rectification, see Norman 2007: 196. The translation here follows Dhammapala in glossing *abhisaṃviseyyaṃ* by *abhiniviseyyaṃ* (Pruitt 1999: 357).

9 This verse employs Buddhist technical vocabulary that is used to describe the objective nature of a person: *khanda,* the five aggregates (constituents of a person), *dhātu,* the elements (constituents of being), and *āyatana,* sense-base. Saying that all of these things are constructed (*saṅkhataṃ*) indicates that objectively each is dependent on something else for its existence and that subjectively they are misconstrued through our mental constructions as an autonomous being.

10 That is, in the six places for rebirth in Buddhist cosmology.

11 The Buddha. See the note to v. 460.

12 The translation is guided by Dhammapala. When the palmyra palm is cut to a stump, it will not send up new shoots, so effectively it is dead. See Norman 2007: 201 and Pruitt 1999: 360 for the textual difficulties of the simile.

13 There are problems with the form of *vāraṇavate,* which are discussed by Norman 2007: 202, and various emendations to the text have been suggested by Alsdorf and Norman. The translation here follows Dhammapala, who in his contextual prologue to the poem of Sumedha says that her parents had decided to give her in marriage to Anikadatta in the city of Varanavati (Pruitt 1999: 343).

14 The first *jhāna,* that experience, or actually that abolition of experience, that is the result of meditations that withdraw the

practitioner from the world, and even from awareness of the self; they are said to be like a turtle withdrawing into its shell.

15 Repeating what her parents had said to her.

16 There is a pun here; it also means "the kingdom has been given up by you."

17 A primeval king who could have any pleasure or object that he wanted in this world.

18 Dhammapala explains that people break the limbs of a tree while trying to get the fruits (Pruitt 1999: 364).

19 A mountain outside Rajagaha.

20 Dhammapala (Pruitt 1999: 369) explains that becoming a "crocodile" represents, metaphorically, gluttony and thus the attractions of returning to lay life.

21 There is word play here on *amata* as ambrosia and as the deathless, that is, nibbana.

22 One for each of the physical senses.

23 For "constructed," see notes to vv. 391 and 475.

24 The translation here of *sokabhayabhītā* follows Dhammapala's gloss, who explains that Sumedha was frightened (*bhītā*) by a fear (*bhaya*) of samsara that is the cause of being separated from relatives and other sorrows (*soka*) (Pruitt 1999: 373).

25 That is, she became enlightened. For six higher powers, see Glossary, s.v. *Chaḷabhiññā*.

26 A Buddha who lived in an eon previous to the one in which we live.

GLOSSARY

ĀSAVA the depravities that ooze out from within. In Buddhist psychology, these are features of corrupting dispositions of being that befoul our minds, like discharges from a sore. Freedom from these depravities is a contour of enlightenment. These are often linked with other latent dispositions in our moral psychology, such as the *kilesa*.

ĀYATANA the senses and their objects in a single continuum. In Buddhist psychology of perception, a single term, *āyatana,* covers both the senses (five physical senses and the mind as a sixth sense) and those things in the world known through the senses. The *āyatana* thus are the subjective and objective poles of sensory experience held together in one continuum. These are often joined in one concatenation with *khanda* and *dhātu*.

CHAḶABHIÑÑĀ six powers beyond normal that allow one to have direct knowledge of things that otherwise are not known. These powers are (1) possessing the divine eye, (2) the divine ear, (3) psychic powers, (4) knowledge of other people's thoughts, (5) recollection of former existences, and (6) knowledge of the destruction of the depravities that ooze out from within, the *āsavas*.

DHAMMA the Pali equivalent of the Sanskrit word Dharma. Dhamma refers both to what the Buddha taught and to the nature of reality as it truly is. The nature of reality as it truly is, as distinguished from how it is conventionally perceived, is what the Buddha taught. The Buddha's dhamma, his teaching, is not only true in what it says about the world but it is also useful in helping humans to free themselves from the world of suffering that they find themselves in.

DHĀTU the basic elements that make up everything. The *dhātu* are the primary elements of all that exists, and a conventional set of them consists of earth, water, fire, and wind. They are often joined in one concatenation with *khanda* and *āyatana*.

EIGHTFOLD PATH the way of life taught by the Buddha, made up of eight elements: right views, right aspirations, right speech, right conduct, right livelihood, right effort, right mindfulness, and right concentration.

FOUR NOBLE TRUTHS the basic teachings of the Buddha, but also in the sense of established facts. The four noble truths are (1) that the character of everything is unsatisfactory, and thus, "all this is suffering"; (2) this unsatisfactoriness has an origin, namely in desire; (3) there is an end to this unsatisfactoriness; and (4) there is a way to this ending of unsatisfactoriness in the way of life taught by the Buddha, encapsulated in the noble eightfold path.

GOTAMA a lineage name of the Buddha's that indicates the line of descent of which he was part.

JHĀNA a meditative state of profound concentration in which the mind becomes absorbed in increasingly rarified objects of attention. A Buddhist technical term for special kinds of religious experience, the *jhānas* are ordered in a sequence of four, based on the achievement of increasing absorption in meditation.

KHANDA what makes a person, the basic constituents of a person. They are five, together a concatenation of things and events: physical things, as in the body; feelings; perceptions; innate dispositions; and consciousness. These things, bundled together (*khanda*), constitute a person, each *khanda* co-dependent with the others, the parts and whole of a person constantly changing. To perceive oneself in such terms is conducive to freedom from the mental constructions that one has of oneself. These are often joined in one concatenation with *āyatana* and *dhātu*.

KILESA defiling compulsions. Like the *āsavas*, the kilesa are latent dispositions that drive our actions in ways that we cannot foresee or control. Among these defiling compulsions are passion, anger, delusion, and craving.

MARA the personification of death and evil, often portrayed in the *Therīgāthā* as a tempter to the *therīs*, looking for an opportunity to undermine their sense of achievement.

NIBBĀNA the Pali equivalent of nirvana. Nibbana is the freedom and happiness attained by humans who learn to live as the Buddha taught. The words nibbana and nirvana both come from a verbal root meaning "to blow out" and this metaphor refers to the "fires" of desire (especially the urge for sex), anger, and ignorance burning out and ceasing to be. Nibbana happens when the *āsavas*, the depravities that ooze out from within, and the *kilesas*, latent and defiling compulsions that drive actions, are removed. The person who attains nibbana subsequently lives a life of freedom and happiness and, at death, is not reborn again.

PUÑÑA the merit produced by intentional good actions, such as being generous to Buddhist monks and nuns. This merit improves one's general store of good karma, and it can also be dedicated or transferred to someone else.

TEVIJJĀ the three things that most people do not know. These are the ability to know one's past lives; the ability to know where and why other beings are reborn; and the ability to know one's own moral corruptions—"all that holds one back"—have been eliminated. To know the three things that most don't know is to know that one is enlightened and that one will not be reborn. The notion of *tevijjā* in early Buddhism explicitly triggers association with ideas in Brahmanical Hinduism about *trayī vidyā,* knowledge of the three Vedas. When the *therīs* declare that they know the three things that most don't know, they are not only making a joyful affirmation of the attainment, they are rejecting Brahmanical assumptions that no woman of any caste was capable of attaining "the three knowledges."

BIBLIOGRAPHY

Editions and Translations

Access to Insight. 2011. "Therigāthā" (Thi_utf8). http://www.accesstoinsight.org/tipitaka/sltp/Thi_utf8.html. Retrieved on 14 July 2013.

Access to Insight. 2012. "Therigatha: Verses of the Elder Nuns." *Access to Insight*. http://www.accesstoinsight.org/tipitaka/kn/thig/. Retrieved on 14 July 2013.

Bhagwat, N. K., ed. 1939. *Therīgāthā: Pourings of Verse of the Buddhist bhikkhuṇis*. Bombay: University of Bombay. (Devanagari-Pali Text Series.) 2nd ed., 1956.

Bihalpola Siri Dewarakkhita Thera, ed., and revised by Mahagoda Siri Nanissara Thera. 1918. *Paramattha Dīpanī or the Commentary of the Therigatha*. Colombo: Tripitaka Publication Press. (Simon Hewavitarne Bequest Series). Reprinted 1985 (Somawati Hewavitarane Trust).

Bodhi, Bhikkhu, trans. 2000. *The Connected Discourses of the Buddha: A Translation of the* Saṃyutta Nikāya. Boston: Wisdom Publications.

Carter, John Ross and Mahinda Palihawadana, trans. 2000. *The Dhammapada: Sayings of the Buddha*. (Oxford World's Classics.) Oxford: Oxford University Press.

De Zoysa, A. P., trans. 1956. *Khuddakanikāya 2: Petavatthu, Theragāthā, Therīgāthā, Jātaka*. Colombo: Dharmasamaya.

Feer, Léon, ed. 1884. *The Saṃyutta-nikāya of the Sutta-piṭaka*. Vol. 1. London: Pali Text Society.

Halgastota Dewananda Thera, ed. 1970. *The Therigatha Pali of Suttanta Pitaka*. Colombo: Tripitaka Publication Press.

Horner, I. B., trans. 1963. *Milinda's Questions*. (Sacred Books of the Buddhists, vol. 22.) London: Luzac, for the Pali Text Society.

Huabdee, Kritchada and Sathienpong Wannapok, trans. 1988; 2nd ed., 2005. *The Songs of the Arahants*. Bangkok: Ariyamagga Foundation.

Jayawickrama, N. A., ed. 1958. *Therīgāthā vyākhyā*. Colombo: M. D. Gunasena.

Karahampitigoda Sumanasara Thera, ed. 1972. *Therīgāthā Pāḷi*. Colombo: Lanka Bauddha Mandalaya. (Buddha Jayanti Tripitaka Series.) Digital version available at: http://gretil.sub.uni-goettingen.de/gretil.htm#Tipit. Retrieved on 14 July 2013.

Kashyap, Bhikkhu J., ed. 1959. *The Vimānavatthu-Petavatthu-Theragāthā-Therīgāthā* (Khuddanikāya Vol. II). N.p.: Pāli Publication Board. (Nalanda Devanagari Pali Series.)

Majumdar, Bijay Chandra, trans. [1905]. *Therīgāthā*. Dacca: Srihemendranatha Datta.

Masefield, Peter, trans. 1994. *The Udāna Commentary (Paramatthadīpanī nāma Udānaṭṭhakathā) by Dhammapāla*. (Sacred Books of the Buddhists, vol. 43.) Oxford: Pali Text Society.

Masset, Danièle, trans. 2005. *Stances des* Therī. Oxford: Pali Text Society.

Müller, Edward, ed. 1893. *Paramatthadīpanī* [V] *Dhammapāla's Commentary on the Therīgāthā*. London: Pali Text Society.

Murcott, Susan, trans. 1991. *The First Buddhist Women: Translations and Commentary on the* Therigatha. Berkeley: Parallax Press.

Neumann, Karl Eugen, trans. 1899. *Die Lieder der Mönche und Nonnen Gotamo Buddho's*. Berlin: Ernst Hofmann.

Norman, K. R., trans. 1969. *The Elders' Verses I Theragāthā*. London: Pali Text Society. 2nd ed., 2007.

———, trans. 2007. *The Elders' Verses II Therīgāthā*. 2nd ed. London: Pali Text Society. 1st ed., 1971.

Obeyesekere, Ranjini, trans. 2001. *Portraits of Buddhist Women: Stories from the* Saddharmaratnāvaliya. Albany: State University of New York Press.

Pischel, Richard, ed. 1883. *Therīgāthā*. London: Pali Text Society; 2nd ed., with an appendix by L. Alsdorf, 1966.

Pruitt, William, ed. 1998. *Therīgāthā-aṭṭhakathā* (*Paramatthadīpanī VI*.) Oxford: Pali Text Society.

———, trans. 1999. *The Commentary on the Verses of the Therīs*. Oxford: Pali Text Society.

Rhys Davids, Mrs. [Caroline A. F.], trans. 1909. *Psalms of the Early Buddhists I. Psalms of the Sisters*. London: Pali Text Society.

Rhys Davids, Mrs. C. A. F. and K. R. Norman, trans. 1989. *Poems of Early Buddhist Nuns* (*Therīgāthā*). Oxford: Pali Text Society. (Revised versions of Rhys Davids 1909 and Norman 1971.)

S. Nanavarabharana Thera, ed. 1927 (B.E. 2470.) *Suttantapiṭake Khuddakanikāyassa Vimānavatthu-Petavatthu-Theragāthā-Therīgāthā*. Bangkok: Mahamakuta Raja Vidyalaya Press. (Syāmaraṭṭhassa tepīṭaṃ; Second Siamese Edition of the Tipitaka.) Digital version available at: http://www.mahidol.ac.th/budsir/budsir-main.html. Retrieved on 14 July 2013.

Sankrityayan, Rahul, ed. 1937. *Therīgāthā*. Rangoon: Uttamabhikkhu.

Schelling, Andrew and Anne Waldman, trans. 1996. *Songs of the Sons and Daughters of Buddha*. Boston: Shambala Publications.

Sri Dharmakirti Dhammananda, ed. 1926. *Therīgāthā pāli*. Colombo: Buddhist Students Union.

Sutantapitak khuddakanikay theragatha therigatha. 1959 (B.E. 2502). Phnom Penh: (Tripitaka Khmer).

Suttantapiṭake Khuddakanikāye Vimānavatthu, Petavatthu, Theragāthā, Therīgāthāpāḷi. 1955. Rangoon: Sasana Council of Burma. 3rd ed., 1961. Reprinted 2005. (Chatthasangiti pitakam.) Reprinted 1993.

Suttantapiṭake Khuddakanikāye Vimānavatthupāḷi, Petavatthupāḷi, Theragāthāpāḷi, Therigāthāpāḷi. 1998. Igatpuri: Vipassana Research Institute. (Dhammagiri Pali ganthamala.) Digital version available at: http://www.tipitaka.org/index.shtml. Retrieved on 14 July 2013.

Tharu, Susie J. and K. Lalita, eds. 1991. *Women Writing in India: 600 B.C. to the Present*. New York: Feminist Press at the City University of New York.

Upadhyaya, Bharatsimha, trans. 1950. *Therīgāthāeṃ: bhikshuṇiyoṃ ke bhāvanā-pūrṇa udāra*. New Delhi: Sasta Sahitya Mandala.

Wickramasinghe, Martin, trans. 1992. In Mārṭin Vikramasiṃha kṛti ekatuva, Volume 8. *Tērigī*. Dehiwala, Sri Lanka: Tisara. 1st ed., 1952.

Other Sources

Analayo, Bhikkhu. 2012. "Beautiful Eyes Seen with Insight as Bereft of Beauty: Subhā Therī and Her Male Counterpart in the Ekottarika Āgama." *The Sati Journal, The Journal for the Sati Center for Buddhist Studies* 2: 1–5.

Bartholomeusz, Tessa. 1994. *Women under the Bo Tree*. Cambridge: Cambridge University Press.

Blackstone, Kathryn R. 1998. *Women in the Footsteps of the Buddha: Struggle for Liberation in the Therīgāthā*. Richmond: Curzon Press.

Bode, Mabel. 1893. "Women Leaders of the Buddhist Reformation." *Journal of the Royal Asiatic Society* 25: 517–566, 763–798.

Bronkhorst, Johannes. 2007. *Greater Magadha: Studies in the Culture of Early India*. (Handbook of Oriental Studies, Section Two: India, vol. 19.) Leiden: E.J. Brill.

Choubey, Asha. 2009. "Voices from Yore: Therigatha Writings of the Bhikkhunis." *The Indian Review of World Literature in English* 5: 1–9.

Collett, Alice. 2006. "Buddhism and Gender, Reframing and Refocusing the Debate." *Journal of Feminist Studies in Religion* 22: 55–84.

———, ed. 2013. *Women in Early Indian Buddhism*. New York: Oxford University Press.

COLLINS, STEVEN. 1982. *Selfless Persons: Imagery and Thought in* Theravāda *Buddhism*. Cambridge: Cambridge University Press.

———. 2000. "The Body in Theravāda Buddhist Monasticism." In *Religion and the Body*, ed. Sarah Coakley. Cambridge: Cambridge University Press, pp. 185–204.

———. 2003. "What Is Literature in Pali?" In *Literary Cultures from South Asia: Reconstructions from History*, ed. Sheldon Pollock. Berkeley: University of California Press, pp. 649–688.

DHADPALE, M. G. 1975. *Some Aspects of (Buddhist) Literary Criticism as Gleaned from Pali Sources*. Bombay: Adreesh Prakashan.

GOMBRICH, RICHARD. 1988. *Theravada Buddhism: A Social History from Ancient Benares to Modern Colombo*. London: Routledge and Kegan Paul.

———. 1990. "A Note on Ambapāli's Wit." *Journal of the Pali Text Society* 15: 139–140.

HAMILTON, SUE. 2000. *Early Buddhism: A New Approach. The Eye of the Beholder*. Richmond, Surrey: Curzon.

HARDY, FRIEDHELM. 1994. *The Religious Culture of India: Power, Love and Wisdom*. Cambridge: Cambridge University Press.

HECKER, HELLMUTH. 1972–1976. *Buddhist Women at the Time of the Buddha*. Trans. by Sister Khema. http://bhikkhuni.net/library/hecker-ancient-buddhist-women.html. Retrieved on 14 July 2013.

HORNER, I. B. 1930. *Women Under Primitive Buddhism*. London: George Routledge and Sons.

———. 1963. *Early Buddhist Poetry*. Colombo: Ananda Semage.

KLOPPENBORG, RIA. "Female Stereotypes in Early Buddhism: The Women of the Therīgāthā." In *Female Stereotypes in Religious Traditions*, ed. Ria Kloppenborg and Wouter J. Hanegraaff. Leiden: E.J. Brill, pp. 151–169.

LANG, KAREN. 1986. "Lord Death's Snare: Gender-Related Imagery in the *Theragāthā* and the *Therīgāthā*." *Journal of Feminist Studies in Religion* 2: 63–79.

LIENHARD, SIEGFRIED. 1975. "Sur la structure poétique des Theratherīgāthā." *Journal Asiatique* 263: 375–396.

OLIVIA, NONA [SARANA]. 2011. "Learning from the Therīgāthā: What

Liberated the Venerable Nun Uttama." *The Sati Journal, The Journal for the Sati Center for Buddhist Studies* 1: 13–23.

POLLOCK, SHELDON. 1977. *Aspects of Versification in Sanskrit Lyric Poetry*. (American Oriental Series 61.) New Haven, Conn.: American Oriental Society.

———. 2006. *The Language of the Gods in the World of Men*. Berkeley: University of California Press.

POUND, EZRA. 1960. *The ABC of Reading*. New York: New Directions Publishing.

RAJAPAKSE, VIJITHA. 1995. "Therīgāthā: On Feminism, Aestheticism and Religiosity in an Early Buddhist Verse Anthology." *Buddhist Studies Review* 12: 7–26, 135–155.

SPONBERG, ALAN. 1992. "Attitudes Toward Women and the Feminine in Early Buddhism." In *Buddhism, Sexuality, and Gender*, ed. José Cabezón. Albany: State University of New York Press, pp. 3–36.

TRAINOR, KEVIN. 1993. "In the Eye of the Beholder: Nonattachment and the Body in Subhā's Verse (Therīgāthā 71)." *Journal of the American Academy of Religion* 61: 57–79.

VON HINÜBER, OSKAR. 1996. *A Handbook of Pāli Literature*. Berlin: de Gruyter.

WARDER, A. K. 1967. *Pali Metre: A Contribution to the History of Indian Literature*. London: Pali Text Society.

WIJAYARATNA, MOHAN. 2010. *Buddhist Nuns*. Kandy, Sri Lanka: Buddhist Publication Society.

WILLEMEN, CHARLES, BART DESSEIN, and COLLETT COX. 1998. *Sarvāstivāda Buddhist Scholasticism*. Leiden: Brill.

WINTERNITZ, M. 1987. *History of Indian Literature: Buddhist Literature*, trans. Bhaskara Jha. Delhi: Bharatiya Vidya Prakashan.

WRIGHT, J. C. 1999. "Old Wives' Tales in Therīgāthā: A Review Article." *Bulletin of the School of Oriental and African Studies* 62: 519–528.

YAMAZAKI, MORIICHI and YUMI OUSAKA. 2000. *A Pāda Index and Reverse Pāda Index to Early Pāli Canonical Texts: Suttanipāta, Dhammapada, Theragāthā, and Therīgāthā*. Tokyo: Kosei Publishing.

INDEX

ABOUT THE BOOK

Murty Classical Library of India volumes are designed by Rathna Ramanathan and Guglielmo Rossi. Informed by the history of the Indic book and drawing inspiration from polyphonic classical music, the series design is based on the idea of "unity in diversity," celebrating the individuality of each language while bringing them together within a cohesive visual identity.

The Pali and English texts are set in Antwerp, designed by Henrik Kubel from A2-TYPE and chosen for its versatility and balance with the Indic typography. The design is a free-spirited amalgamation and interpretation of the archives of type at the Museum Plantin-Moretus in Antwerp.

All the fonts commissioned for the Murty Classical Library of India will be made available, free of charge, for non-commercial use. For more information about the typography and design of the series, please visit *http://www.hup.harvard.edu/mcli.*

Printed on acid-free paper by Maple Press, York, Pennsylvania.